Evolution: The BIG Lie!

The "theory" that has never been proven and can't be, here's why.

By
Kenneth Edward Barnes

The author, standing on a giant sycamore tree along Cypress Creek, in Warrick County, Indiana. The tree was over twenty-nine feet in circumference.

The cover photo was taken by me and is of an Eastern Box Turtle.

This turtle has been coming to our house for over 20 years as of 2019. It is a female and has been seen digging a nest and laying eggs on the property. I first saw her in 1998 and gave her a small piece of cantaloupe. Since then she has remembered and has come back every summer for more treats. She loves cantaloupe, watermelon, strawberries and hotdogs.

When I first saw her, she was so old that the spots on her shell were nearly worn off. She still looks the same, so there is no telling how old she is. She could well be over a hundred years old, perhaps much older!

Animals are not as dumb as many believe. This old turtle proves this. She remembered that she was given something she had never tasted before and she has returned every year since. She will even let me or my wife, Lilly, hold her and will eat while we are doing so. Other turtles have also come to the house looking for a treat after they have been fed only once. Several of them have come to be fed, including one Lilly named "Big Orange" because he is a large male and bright orange. His photo is below. They

2

often wait next to the porch until we see them and give them something. When we see them waiting, they will look up at us and stay there until we get them a treat they like. Once they're full, they head back into the forest.

Contents

Prologue

Most believe that evolution is a fact. The fact is, it is still a theory and has never been proven. I have studied nature since childhood and I'm an outdoor writer. I have also studied the Bible for well over fifty years. Therefore, there are only two possible truths. Either everything that exist came about by blind chance without rhyme or reason or there is a God that created it for a specific purpose.

In this book, I will give some startling facts that show that evolution could not possibly account for the complex variety of life. I will also give some Bible verses, which show that God is the Creator and that those that believe in evolution must have "faith" in a world that has created itself.

In writing this book, which is contains about 27,000 words, I will be using some quotes and a couple of excerpts from several of my other books already written.

Some of what is in this book is from the commentary about evolution at the end of my book, *Christ: His Words, His Life* and some text is from *Mysteries of the Bible.* Much of it, however, is new and there are many quotes from the Bible explaining the creation of our world and its creatures, as this is where the greatest controversy lies.

As I said above, you only have *two* choices to believe in. Either God created the universe and all that is in it, including life, or by some "magic" it came into being all by itself. Einstein was smarter than most of us will ever be and he believed God had to create the universe because it is far too complex and everything obeys physical laws and is in order. This is not strange because the Bible says "God is not the author of confusion, but of peace…" This means He is a God of order.

I have studied nature since I was a child, which is over sixty years now. Even during elementary school, I would often spend my study time reading encyclopedias about prehistoric birds and animals. Once, I had to give a speech in front of the sixth-grade class about any topic of our choice. I chose to do it about dinosaurs. I talked for several minutes about many different kinds of these prehistoric serpents. I told my classmates how much each kind weighed, their length, height, and other facts peculiar to their kind. After the speech, the teacher was so impressed with my knowledge and memory of all the different species that she told other teachers about it. It just so happened that the third-grade class was studying dinosaurs. I was then asked to come to their classroom and give a speech about all I knew about them.

Since that time, I have studied not only prehistoric birds and animals, but also all wildlife. As a boy and young man, Abraham Lincoln lived just a little way up Little Pigeon Creek from where I was born. In addition, like him, I did a lot of reading and studying on my own, so I feel I am in good company.

Surprising, many Christians believe in evolution, and many also believe that the world is only six thousand years old; both are wrong. I explain why and quote what the Bible says and not what others think it says. Therefore, you will be able to read for yourselves and make up your own mind.

I have also studied the Bible since I was fourteen, which was back in 1965. I am writing this book to help explain some facts that I believe prove that evolution is a lie, yes, a BIG lie. No, evolution could not "create" by blind chance, by hit and miss gene mutations, or by trial and error, the great perfection we see in nature. I believe those that want to know real science and not "theories" that claim to be true, without being proven, can read for themselves and see another view. If God is the Creator, then we need to look to Him for the answers. For if He did not create us and all life, then nothing in the universe matters. It does not matter if everything just happened by accident or by a series of bizarre coincidences, because when we die everything will be over. In that case, we should not worry about anything. We should just make up our own rules and take what we can by any means possible. Just eat, drink and be merry, for tomorrow we may die. Oh, I'm sorry, those are words from the Bible of how people will be just before Christ's second coming, Luke, 12:19 and Matthew, 24:37. This sounds like many people today, doesn't it?

Chapter 1

This is a Polyphemus moth, and it shows that God has a sense of humor

Before Darwin

Before Darwin, most people believed in creation in one form or another, by either one God or many gods. They could see all the different plants, animals, the moon, stars, oceans, and mountains, and thought there had to be some intelligent being behind the scene that made it all.

The "scientists" that lived a couple of hundred years before the "theory" of evolution was popular, had already divided animals into classes. They did this by simple observation and had much of it correct. As time went on and more knowledge was gained, they were able to separate the species much better. The first time that a duckbill platypus skin from Australia was sent to Europe, it was believed to be a prank. They thought this because the animal was unlike anything that had ever been seen before. It was believed that someone had skillfully sewn several parts of different animals together. The platypus and the echidna, or spiny anteater, are the only monotremes in the world, which means they are mammals that lay eggs.

Because of increased knowledge and many discoveries over the years, scientists have had to change many long-held beliefs about classes of animals. Many times, they had it all wrong. Only recently, a "scientist" discovered a "primitive human tooth", only to later find that it belonged to a pig! Just in my lifetime, the giant panda was considered to be a bear, then not a bear, but more closely related to the raccoon, and now, once again, it is classified as a bear.

With genetic testing, many birds and animals are being found to be related to other species that is not very obvious. From what I have heard, genetics has showed that vultures *are not* related to birds of prey, but are more closely related to storks. This sounds logical, for if you look at a marabou stork or several other kinds of storks, they have a naked head as do vultures. Vultures also do not have talons as do birds of prey in which to tear apart animals. Often, they must wait for birds of prey or other scavenging animals to tear into a carcass of a dead animal before they can eat. They also have a bare head so that when the reach into a carcass they will not get blood on any feathers and the sun can dry their bald head much easier. Yes, there is a reason for everything in nature.

I'm also sure that as time goes on, more and more discoveries, especially genetic mapping, will reveal other mysteries of animal relationships and some will have to be re-classified.

Not long after Darwin proposed the "theory" of birds and animals slowly evolving from lower forms to much more advanced forms, it was widely accepted as scientific fact. Darwin, like many others, assumed that over time many "missing links" would be discovered that would prove him correct. This has not happened. In fact, there have been more questions raised than answered by what scientists have discovered. Darwin could not even have imagined how complicated a living organism is. He knew nothing of genetic DNA and how unbelievably complicated a simple sequence is for the tiniest thing in an animal. Just the DNA sequence for the flash of a firefly takes over 20 feet of code! This is only one small part of this insect. It has much more DNA sequences for everything, from its eyes, breathing, wings, external skeleton, digestive system, reproductive system, and blood, not to mention the preprogrammed instinct for

11

moving, flying, mating, eating, and so forth. This is *just one* insect and there may be as many as one million different insects on earth. Then there are the birds, animals, crustaceans, arachnids, worms, and countless plants.

On the surface, evolution *sounds logical*. If you look closer, however, you will soon see that it is riddled with gaps so great that it takes a giant leap of faith to believe it is even remotely possible.

I have read that near the end of his life, Darwin had doubts himself about evolution. He also said something to this effect, "If evolution were true, then everything would be in constant confusion from changing into more advanced creatures."

Every creature on earth is "designed" perfectly to be able to live in its environment; to gather its food, find shelter, and to find a mate with which to reproduce. I will give some examples later of just how ridiculous it would be for an animal to change into a different creature when it is already perfectly suited for the life it has. Moreover, this is after the creature is already here, let alone evolving it from scratch.

There may be a word that describes a living organism that has to have everything in place and all at the same time to be alive and/or to function property, but I have never heard of one. If there is no such word, I believe we need one that would describe much better the complex and "intelligent design" that created all life than the "theory of evolution". As I said, I have never heard of such a word, but I think it should be called the ***"omni-theory"***. If there is no such word, there is now. My *omni-theory* states: All elements necessary for life must be present at the same time for that life form to exist and to function properly.

Chapter 2

A giant tortoise on one of the Galapagos Islands where Darwin studied nature.

Darwin's Evaluation

Charles Robert Darwin was born in 1809. He died in 1882, and was a naturalist from Britain. Sailing in a ship, called the Beagle, Darwin traveled many places on earth studying plants and animals. He also came to the Galapagos Islands where he found and studied many species of birds and animals. He later wrote the book "The Origin of

Species". He believed, by his observations, that "natural selection" or "survival of the fittest" was responsible for the rise of different species from a lower and more primitive life form. He surmised that if a plant or animal has some small variation that favored it to survive in its environment better than its parents or siblings then this trait would be passed on to future generations. Then, over time, all these tiny changes would give rise to different species. This sounded logical. Birds and animals, as well as plants, have been domesticated for centuries. There are hundreds of different breeds of dogs, cats, chickens, pigeons, ducks, geese, horses, cows, sheep, goats and pigs. This is not to mention all the different varieties of plants we use for food. One set of parents can give rise to many different breeds because of slight variations of the offspring.

I have raised many breeds of chickens, pigeons, ducks, geese, sheep and goats. I have owned many breeds of dogs and cats. I have also studied wildlife since childhood and have seen several gene mutations among wild birds and animals. I have seen white blackbirds, albino deer and squirrels. I have seen several species of birds and animals with partial albinism: white tail feathers on grackles; a white-headed blue jay; white spotted blackbirds and sparrows. I've seen European starlings that had blonde tail-feathers or were totally blonde colored. I once saw a house sparrow that was white with gold wing patches, which gave me the inspiration to write a book called *In Search of a Golden Sparrow*. I later found with this white sparrow, one that was all gold colored. I once had a raccoon that had two of its hind toes fused together. When I was a boy, I once saw a horse that had an extra hoof on its front leg. I have also seen two-headed snakes and turtles.

One of the oddest dogs I ever saw was one that an uncle gave me. The dog was born without a tail. It had only a two-inch stump instead of a normal tail and looked as if it had been cut off. This was odd enough, but what was even stranger, was that when it "wagged" its tail, or what tail he had, it did not go from side-to-side as a normal dog, but instead went up and down!

None of this is new; gene mutations have been going on since life began. This is how we have been able to breed different birds, animals and plants to get desirable traits for our own benefit. All races of humans came from only two parents. This has been proven by DNA (do a search for "the Eve gene"). We have been breeding creatures for centuries by selecting traits we want, but in all these centuries we have not once come up with one different specie. There are dozens of different breeds of dogs in all shapes and sizes, but they are still a dog. All will breed with one another and the offspring will still be a dog. There is a great variation among dogs but there is also a limit. Even with selective breeding, you cannot get a two-thousand-pound dog. You may be able to get a two-thousand-pound cow, horse, or several other wild animals if you selectively breed them, but not a dog no matter how much you try. The same goes for a domestic cat. If one "cat ancestor" gave rise to the house cat, the leopard, cheetah, jaguar, lion and tiger, you would think that we should be able to selectively breed a house cat over time to get a tiger. We cannot even get one to look exactly like a tiger, lion, or cheetah, let alone to be the size of one. Each species has a "built-in" program that sets limits on size, shape and color.

I have raised the gorgeous Lady Amherst pheasant and the spectacular golden pheasant. It would be wonderful if we could get the colors of these pheasants into some of the breeds of chickens. After all, chickens *are* a type of pheasant. Gallus gallus gallus is the scientific name of the subspecies of red junglefowl that most believe is the ancestor of the domestic chicken (therefore, if you have ever eaten chicken you can say you have eaten pheasant). However, even though the domestic chicken is a pheasant and a close relative of the two pheasants I have mentioned above, breeders cannot get the bright red, blue or yellow that these pheasants have. These colors are coded in the genes. The genes limit size, shape, color and many other factors in an animal.

Man has bred animals by selecting traits he wants and has come up with some interesting breeds. This, however, has not always proved wise. The English bulldog is so deformed that it has trouble breathing; it cannot clean itself properly; it cannot even have offspring naturally without running the risk of death. Several breeds of birds and animals are so large that they cannot breed naturally and must have artificial insemination to reproduce. These would have never survived in the wild.

All this is by man's forethought and "intelligence" when he is trying to "improve" on what nature has done. Just think of "blind chance" creating any kind of creature.

In order for an animal to fit into its environment, it has to have all the necessary adaptations for survival. I can just see a turtle saying to himself, "Hey, I'm tired of being in the water; I think I will go on land and become a tortoise." If he stayed out too long his shell would crack because of the dry conditions; he would also find it difficult to locate food. Then, if he survived long enough, he could not find a mate because no other turtles were dumb enough to follow him.

According to *The World Book Encyclopedia* 1990 edition, it says, "During the first half of the 1900's, discoveries in genetics and developmental biology were used as evidence for theories of evolution that regarded natural selection as unimportant." This disproved the very thing that started the debate. Darwin's theory of "natural selection" the "survival of the fittest" was **proved not to be true**. "Then, after world War II ended in 1945, Darwin's theories again became the dominant influence in evolutionary biology in a form often called Neo-Darwinism." After this, "in the 1960s, discoveries in molecular biology and paleontology have been used to support non-Darwinian theories of evolution."

Many do not know that Hitler was influenced by Darwin and that was the reason he believed that the German race was superior and other races we inferior. Because of this, he tortured, starved, and murdered multiple millions of human beings thinking they needed to be weeded out.

It seems that those that believe in evolution still cling to the theory in one form or another. Even when some parts of the theory are disproved, they cannot let go of their "faith" that it has to be true. Why is this? One main reason is that if evolution is proved to be a lie, then those that believed that everything happened by random chance will have to have "another theory" to explain creation without a Supreme Being. If they accept that God did indeed create everything, including us, then they are faced with the dilemma that He will do what He says He will do in the Holy Bible. This means that they will have to "believe" that God will judge them someday and hold them accountable for what they have done in this life. They will also be faced with the problem and fate of not believing in Him when He showed His power, majesty, and wisdom in His creation.

It is interesting to note that every theory is just that, a theory until it is proved to be fact, *except* for evolution. Every theory that scientists come up with must be tested over and over. It must be proven beyond any doubt before it can be accepted as fact. At least every theory but one and that is evolution. Nearly from the beginning of its conception, the theory of evolution was viewed as being fact by most scientists. Later, when there was other evidence that the foundation of this "belief" was not true, the theory was still considered as fact.

Over the centuries, many theories have come about, such as the earth being round, gravity, the speed of light and many others. They cannot be, however, taken as fact until they are proven. As I said, a theory must be proven so that there is no possibility that the theory is flawed, that it is indeed the correct assumption. Evolution has never been proven and cannot be because *it is false.* Anyone with common sense can examine things for themselves.

When "experts" try to explain "human evolution" they use phrases such as "perhaps", maybe" or "we think it happened this way". This is because they have to guess at what they think "could have" taken place.

I mentioned Hitler earlier and it was directly because of Darwin's theory of "the survival of the fittest" that Adolph Hitler wanted to breed a "superior race." It was why he "believed" that he had the "right" to commit genocide and kill multiple millions of innocent human beings; six million of them being Jews. Christ himself, our Savior, the one that died for us and gave us the possibility of eternal life, was a Jew. The Apostil Paul said in Romans, 3:1-2, *"What advantage has a Jew? Much in every way, because unto them were committed the oracles of God."*

Because Hitler "believed this lie"; the "theory" that one race was superior than another, he felt he could make up his own moral values. I have also just written a book I titled *A Rude Awakening*. I believe this book should be read by every Christian that wishes to know the truth of what will happen just before Christ returns. Just as Hitler did in his time, people today are making up their own moral values and twisting God's word and denying what He really said.

If we believe in evolution, that God had nothing to do with creation, then we are no more than any other animal. In fact, we are worse off than any of the creatures that inhabit this speck of dust in the universe. This is because we have knowledge that we will someday die, which no other animal has. Apostle Paul said in 1 Corinthians, 15:19, "If in this life only we have hope in Christ, we are of all men most miserable." This means that even if we believe in God, but not in a resurrection unto eternal life, we have nothing to look forward to except suffering for doing what is right and not taking the easy road.

God "designed" every creature perfectly for what it does. I love watching nature programs on television. I am also amazed how they give the reason that a certain bird or animal can do extraordinary things. They say things like, "They are *perfectly* adapted." Sometimes they remark, "It's a marvel of evolutionary design!" Other times they even say, "It is a miracle of evolution" or "through the miracle of evolution." The word "design" means that there had to be forethought before something came into being. The word miracle they easily attribute to "blind chance", but not to the One that created it. The Bible says this will happen in the book of Romans. Romans 1:20 states, *"For the invisible things of Him from the creation of the world are clearly seen, being understood by the things that are made, even His eternal power and Godhead, so **they are without excuse**."*

This scripture tells us that we do not need to be a scientist or a genius to know and understand *that the world and its creation could not have just happened by itself.* It tells us that those with common sense can see God in His creation. Romans, 1:22 goes on to say, *"Professing themselves to be wise, they become fools."* Then in verse 25, it says this about these same people,

"Who changed the truth of God into a lie, and **worshipped and served the creature** *more than the Creator…"*

One day, while Christ was preaching about those that were not wanting to find the truth, He said, *"I thank you Father, Lord of heaven and earth, because you have* **hidden these things** *from the wise and prudent and have revealed them unto babes"* (Matthew 11:25).

Also, in 2 Thessalonians, 2:11-12 it says, *"Because of this* (the people who loved not the truth) *God shall send* **strong delusion** *that they* **believe a lie**, *that they all might be damned who believe not the truth, but had pleasure in unrighteousness."*

The Bible here is speaking about the end of time and "the antichrist" who will trick most of the world by his lies into following him. It can also, however, mean *those that reject God as creator* because the same one (Satan) is behind all lies.

An albino gray squirrel. Photo by the author

Chapter 3

The Church and Evolution

In the days *before* Darwin, "the church" was supposed to have the answers to how everything came into being. If you did not believe what they said, you were a heretic and often killed for your belief. Now the pendulum has swung the other way. If you do not believe what most scientists say is truth, you are labeled as being naive, stupid, behind the times or living in a fantasy world. Many scientists that believe in God are not listened to and are often shunned by others in their field. Just as the church of years past jumped to conclusions and believed they knew the truth about how the world was created, so have many scientists today.

During the Dark Ages, you dared not question what "the church" said was true. They knew the earth was flat, even though the Bible does not say so. In fact, the Bible says in in Isaiah, 40:22 that the earth is round. In Job, 26:7, it says, "the earth is hung on nothing." This shows that the earth is suspended in space.

"The church" also said that the earth was the center of the universe and this proved untrue. Many things they read in the Scriptures they read wrong and based their beliefs on. Even now, the majority of Christians believe that Christ died on a Friday and rose Sunday morning, even though Christ himself said differently. He said in Matthew 12:40, that He would give them the "sign of Jonah" and be in the grave "three days and three nights."

Many Christians believe that Christ will catch them away in a "secret rapture" and take them to heaven. They also believe that as soon as a person dies, they will go straight to heaven or hell. Christ said this was not true as did Peter.

Most also believe the earth is only six thousand years old. The Bible does not say this anywhere. Most just jump to conclusions or they take as gospel what they have been told is true. If you wish to understand more about what the Bible truly says about these topics and more, read my books: *A Rude Awakening;* or *Christ: His Words,*

His Life. This last book has all the words Christ spoke in a compilation of the gospels and it has a 33,000-word commentary afterwards. It also has a section about evolution.

Another of my books, *Mysteries of the Bible* is an expanded version of the commentary of the above-mentioned book, but contains around 55,000-words. It goes into more detail about the same topics and has additional insights of the Bible. I have also written many other books about "end time" prophecies.

The leaders of churches are human beings. Humans are not God and they are not infallible as much as they may want you to believe. When Christ was here on earth, He tried to clarify many of the false assumptions that people believed. Even though He gave some very clear and undeniable truths in the gospels, many today dismiss those and take a few passages that can be read differently and base their beliefs on those. If a Scripture is very clear and another is not clear on the same subject, then the obscure one must line up with the one that is easy to understand. If they do not, then you do not have the correct answer.

There is nothing wrong with scientific theories. God is the one that gave man the mind to search and learn. He is the one that created the brain to think, reason and wonder. In fact, He said in His word, "Seek and you shall find; knock and it shall be opened unto you." Here He is talking about the truth. He is speaking about finding the truth of what He says in the Scriptures. It also can be applied to seeking the truth about any subject, even scientific research. He wants people to discover secrets of nature. In one passage, He says, "Doesn't nature itself teach you...?" The Bible also says, "Not one word [of God] will come back void." Even if we do not find all the answers now, He will reveal it someday, even if it is after we come into His kingdom.

If you read the book of Daniel, you will see that God predicted that man would increase greatly in knowledge. Daniel, 12:4 says that near the "time of the end," the time just before Christ returns to earth, that "men shall travel all over the earth and knowledge shall be increased."

God has no fear of us finding out the truth. God fears nothing. He knows the end from the beginning.

If you study the Scriptures, you will see that from the first humans, Adam and Eve, came all the races we now have. If these two people, whom God created, could give rise to different races or families of humans, it is no guess but near certainty that God also did the same with animals. In Adam and Eve's genetic code God would have to have placed all the genes necessary for the different mutations to come to the surface in future generations. Eve was a clone of Adam, only a female. The first children would have to have had to marry one another, as there were no other people on earth. This means the first parents had to be special or there would be serious problems with inbreeding. Later, when the gene pool was diluted by intermarriage, God said they could no longer marry their brother or sister. However, even after the Flood, many married a half-brother or half-sister. Sara was Abraham's half-sister. There are also other instances of this. One is when King David's son, Amnon, raped his half-sister, Tamar. After he committed this sinful act, she wanted him to marry her saying, he had already defiled her and if he didn't marry her it would be a greater sin. The story is in 2 Samuel, Chapter 13.

If you read in Genesis, 6:20, the Bible says that the animals will come to Noah so they can be spared. Noah did not go and gather them to bring them into the ark; God sent them. If God sent them, then God would have to have chosen them. He would have sent the very best with the widest range of genetic diversity so they would not have problems interbreeding. God sent two of each of every unclean animal, but He sent seven of every clean animal. This would have given even more diversity for the prey animals.

We know that many species of animals are related. Some can cross and be fertile; therefore, they must have been the same species at one time. Others can cross and be a hybrid, which cannot reproduce again. The human race is actually comprised of several races but one species and we came from only one set of parents. If God had hundreds of species, which gave rise to all the different birds and animals, we would see thousands of different races, which we do. It is also very possible and probable that God had in these first animals a genetic code that would spin off different species. After they were separated into different species, he set a boundary so they could not cross back and forth. He makes it clear in the Bible that different species are not to cross or even try to do so and calls it "confusion'. This is in Leviticus, 18:23. In Leviticus, 20:12, he says the same thing about people that are too closely related.

God loves variety and this shows in all of his creation. He also has a sense of humor and this can be seen in His creation with some of the strange and often bazar-looking creatures He has made. Most of all, God loves his creation and said, "It is good."

Above is a fox squirrel I raised from a tiny baby. We named him Rufus because he was red. His story is in my book titled *Kenny's Children's Stories*. It is also in *Do Pets go to Heaven?"*

Chapter 4

Take a Close Look at a Feather

According to those that believe in evolution, the complicated structure commonly known as the feather "evolved" from the "scales on a lizard" or some other serpent. They believe that for some unknown reason, a reptile was born with scales that were "frayed" and which kept getting more frayed with each passing generation until it became a feather! How absurd can that be! Have you ever looked closely at a feather? It is very complicated. It has a vane with hundreds of rays running from it. Each ray then has very tiny, microscopic "hooks" that hold the rays into place, much like a zipper does to lock it together. A bird can "unzip" them so it can clean each feather and they will automatically zip back into place. The feather is very lightweight and strong. There are flight feathers on the wings and there are several other feathers on a bird's body. The long feathers, the flight feathers, at the end of a bird's wings are called primary feathers. The ones towards the back of the wing are called secondary feathers. Then you have tail feathers, which are used in steering a bird in flight and to help slow it down. Besides the flight feathers, there are thousands of others, called down, covering a bird's body to keep it warm. Each feather is in a specific location on its body for a specific reason. In many species, there are other feathers just for decoration. The male turkey has feathers on its chest, which are called a "beard" that are long and coarse and feel just like stiff hair. Other birds have elaborate plumes on their head or in their tails just to attract the female. They also know how to display their plumage to attract a potential mate.

There would be no reason for a reptile to grow feathers. Even if it had them, it could not fly. A bird has hollow bones to make it lighter for flight. It has thousands of muscles to move all of its feathers. It has strong pectoral muscles on its breast to give it the strength to operate the wings. In order for a reptile to become a bird, it would have to have thousands of modifications and all at the same time in order to even look like a bird. Besides this, it would also have to have the right kind of brain to know how to use all of the muscles that help it fly.

Retiles are cold-blooded. A bird is warm-blooded. Birds have downy feathers against their skin to keep them warm. Why would a cold-blooded reptile need these kinds of feathers? It would have to first be a warm-blooded creature. If so, it would freeze to death without the downy feathers. It would have to have both at the exact same time.

Now assuming this was even possible, why would it happen? The reptile was doing fine for countless generations being a cold-blooded animal. Then, for no reason, its scales began to change into something it could not use. Downy feathers also began to grow on its cold-blooded body.

You cannot build an automobile a little at a time and expect it to work. You cannot even have most of it built and try to drive it or it will crash and burn. You must have a steering wheel to guide it, tires and wheels to make it move. Brakes to stop it, an engine: all precision made with electrical wires, spark plugs, and a host of electronics to make it run. Then you need a transmission, a differential and hundreds of other parts. After all this, it will sit there forever unless it has gasoline and someone that knows how to drive it. This is an automobile, and an airplane is even more complicated! Moreover, as complicated as a modern jet plane is, the simplest bird is a million times more complicated than the most advanced aircraft.

In order for a reptile to become a bird, there would have to be a "plan" and a "course of action" laid out in advance. All of its parts would have to be there at the same time in order for it to work, just as a jet airplane. There would have to be *intelligent design* to create such a marvelous creature or any kind of animal.

An impressive male, eastern wild turkey from North America. Photo by the author.

Chapter 5

A newly hatched house sparrow.

What About an Egg Tooth?

I have raised chickens and other poultry for many years, and I was always amazed when I saw the "miracle" of an egg hatching. When I first began raising them, I even made a homemade incubator from a cardboard box and a 75-watt light bulb. Later, I bought an incubator and hatched all kinds of eggs. I raised ducks, geese, chickens, pigeons, and Guinea fowl. I also raised several types of game birds such as wood ducks, Mandarin ducks, teal, four kinds of pheasants, three kinds of quail, and chucker partridge. Most of them later hatched their own young.

Everyone has seen an egg. Most have eaten them, either, fried, boiled or scrambled. If you have ever opened a boiled egg you might have noticed that at the large end of the egg there is an airspace. This air pocket is there for a reason. The entire egg is a marvelous creation. It is round, smooth, and is only one cell. An egg is the largest one celled thing on earth. There are also many types of eggs. Amphibians, such as frogs and salamanders have "jelly-like" eggs. Reptile eggs are leathery so they will not break easily, even when dropped in a hole by a turtle.

Birds' eggs are brittle, yet very strong. They must be strong if a bird sits on them for many days or weeks. It takes a lot of pressure to crush an egg by just pushing on the outside. On the inside, however, it takes very little pressure to crack it. This is why it is not too difficult for a tiny chick to peck its way out.

Inside the egg, the little chicken (or other bird) is in a ball. Its legs are against its body and its head is tucked under its wing. If you "candle" an egg, (look at it with a bright light on the far side), you can see the embryo inside. Just a few days after an egg begins incubating the heart of the embryo begins to beat, pumping blood to the rest of the developing chick. A chicken hatches in twenty-one days, twenty if it is very strong.

A day or two before the egg hatches you can hold the egg up to your ear and hear the chick peeping inside. In nature, many eggs from many different species, hatch within minutes of one another. This is true of chickens and other gallinaceous birds. They must all hatch close together so they can leave the nest and follow their mother to find food. Many believe that the chicks inside the eggs hear one another and the chirping and pecking stimulates the others to hatch close together.

Before they hatch, however, they must break through two barriers. The first is a thin membrane inside the egg that separates the chick from the air pocket I mentioned above. If you have seen a hardboiled egg, you might have seen this. This membrane is thin, but strong, especially after it has dried out somewhat from many days of incubation. In order to make it possible to tear through this membrane, a chick has a small "egg tooth" near the end of its beak. This "tooth," which is on top of the beak, is able to rip open this membrane so that it can begin to peck out of the egg. As I said, it is easy to break an egg from the inside. The chick's instincts tell it to peck and it makes a thrust forward with its beak and makes the first break in the eggshell. Usually after the first break in the egg, it will rest a while. Then it will make a second break, a third, fourth and so on. At a certain time, the chick begins to go faster and finishes pecking the egg from the inside and in a circular motion. Its head is tucked under its wing and it must turn inside the egg and go in a circle to complete breaking the end of the egg so it can come out. After it has completed this process, it usually rests a little more. Then, with a strong thrust, it pushes with its legs and shoves itself all the way out. It lies there a while until it feels strong enough to try to stand. In a few hours, the down that covers its body has fluffed out and it can walk.

This is a miracle in itself, but the egg tooth that made it possible to hatch is no longer needed and after three days, it just falls off!

Why would it fall off? It would not harm the bird if it stayed on its beak, for it is very tiny and would wear down in time. It was *designed* for one specific reason and once that reason no longer exists, it is programmed in its DNA to drop off. Evolution would never have created the egg tooth in the first place, and if it did, there would be no reason for it to fall off. This is just one tiny thing that disputes the possibility that creatures could have evolved by hit and miss, by trial and error. Each cell of every creature is perfectly suited for the purpose it is there for. It is mathematically impossible for even one creature to have had all the right things in the right places at the right time and to function flawlessly, let alone millions of creatures that live or that have lived on earth.

I'm sure you've heard the phase, "Like water off a ducks back." Waterfowl such as ducks and geese have an oil gland at the base of their tails.

They take their chin and rub the oil gland then rub the oil all over their feathers. The oil keeps them buoyant in the water and keeps them warm and dry.

So, how did waterfowl "evolve?" They would've had to have the oil gland first before ever getting in the water. They would also have to know how to distribute the oil on their feathers. Why would an oil gland, which is very complicated, suddenly appear on a bird that didn't need it because they never went in the water. Waterfowl can stand bitter cold temperatures and their down is some of the best insulators in the world. Eider down is one example.

No, they could not have "evolved." Every bird, animal or plant that is alive now or that has ever lived is and was perfectly "designed" for how it lived.

Chapter 6

Drawing is from my book:
How to Care for Your MAN
(Mate's Animalistic Needs)

What Are Instincts?

In this chapter is the introduction of my little humorous book **INSTINCTS**, which is an anachronism for *Interesting Natural Secret Tendencies If Nature Could Teach Secrets.* This story is also in a collection with others like it titled *The Book Of HUMOR* and *The B.O. O.K.*

Yes, just what are instincts? Instincts, unlike learned behavior, is knowledge that we have not accumulated over time, but have when we come from the womb. There is some knowledge, however, that higher animals learn in the course of their lives on their own and a few that learn important lessons from watching others of their kind or from their parents. In this book, I will try to show how the "natural" behaviors that we humans are born with affect our lives. How would we behave if we were like other wild animals? What would we eat and how would we find it? How would we attract the opposite sex? In fact, how would we know *how to mate* once a desirable mate was found? Is it instinct or learned behavior? It is nearly impossible to know *exactly* how we would act in every situation if we had only instincts to guide us. However, with careful thought and the research that I have done, we may be able to see fairly clearly, how we would conduct ourselves if we were completely wild and used all the instincts and only the instincts that we were given. After reading, you can draw your own conclusion. I believe that nature can teach us a lot; therefore, here is a look at I.N.S.T.I.N.C.T.S.

In this little book, I tell in a humorous way how we would behave and live if we only had instincts to guide us. At the end of the book, I tell that we are not adapted to this world. This is because unlike all other life forms on earth, we are not equipped with fur, feathers, claws, fangs or can we even run fast or naturally swim to escape our enemies. We cannot find food, defend ourselves without weapons or even build a nest without someone showing us how. We are pretty much helpless if we only relied on our instincts to survive. I say at the end of the book that we do not belong here! I also explain why. It is interesting to note that the Bible says the same thing, *"You are not of this world,"* John 17:16. We were never meant to be like other animals for *we were created in the image of God* and are "the children of God."

Chapter 7

The Little Honeybee

The honeybee is well known to everyone. Bees have been raised for centuries so their honey could be harvested. Before they were raised, honey was found in the wild (and still is) and was prized for its sweetness.

Over the years, it has been discovered that honeybees are remarkable. Not only in making honey out of pollen and nectar, but also in the way their society works. If everything in the hive is not functioning correctly the entire hive's survival is at risk. There are female workers that gather the nectar and pollen. They also produce wax with special glands, which they use to make the comb. Besides this, they must take care of the young, feed the drones, protect the hive and sometimes use their wings to circulate the air in the hive to cool it.

The drones are males and their only function is to mate with a queen and a queen not of their own hive. Drones must be fed by the female honey bees because the drone's tongue is not long enough to gather nectar. It was "designed" this way for a reason. When winter is approaching and food is scarce, the drones are dragged from the hive where they are tossed out to die.

Then there is the queen that lays thousands of eggs (around 2,000 a day) to replenish those bees that die.

Besides producing a substance called royal jelly that turns an ordinary female worker bee into a queen, there are all the intricate social communications that cause the hive to work flawlessly.

As mentioned above, the workers must not only gather the pollen and nectar, they must make the honeycomb. Each cell is so precisely constructed that it was once proposed to be a standard of measurement. It is made to be strong to hold honey, but also to hold the bee larvae inside.

As incredible as all of this is, I believe the most remarkable thing about the bee is its communication system for telling the others where nectar and pollen can be found. A bee that has found a good supply of flowers will perform an elaborate "dance" to tell the other bees where the flowers are, and not only where they are, but how far they are and if there are many or few! In this "waggle dance", it communicates to those bees that have gathered around it in which direction the food source is, how far it is and if it is a small amount or a large amount.

If the bees were not "preprogrammed" to do the dance, or if the others were not "programmed" to interpret it, no information would be transferred and the entire hive would die. If evolution were true, I can just see the first bee that ever did the waggle dance. She is dancing around in a circle, shaking her body while the others go about their business and pay no attention at all. If they did, they would probably think something was wrong with her and perhaps toss her out to die.

Besides all this, the bees' (the workers) stomach is *designed* to take the pollen and change it into honey that they regurgitate. So, when you eat honey, you are eating bee vomit! Could evolution even begin to design a digestive system that could change pollen into vomit that is so tasty and nutritious; not only to them, but to us?

Social insects such as bees, wasps and ants have been here almost from the beginning. After all this time, they look the same and act the same. Ants, bees and other insects have been found in fossilized amber. Some have been estimated to have been there for eighty-million years! You can easily recognize what they are, since they have not changed. The same goes for fossilized leaf prints. An oak leaf still looks like an oak leaf and a maple leaf still looks like a maple leaf even though it "evolved" tens of millions of years ago.

No, there is no way evolution can "think," can "plan," can "design," can come up with all the things necessary for what we see, let alone what is invisible.

Chapter 8

The two beavers above were trapped by a local farmer near my home. The beaver nearly became extinct by the mid-1800s because of over trapping and were gone from my state of Indiana by the 1840s. Restoration efforts by many states have brought them back. Their recovery has been funded by sportsmen's money from hunting, trapping and fishing licenses, along with taxes on outdoor sporting equipment. Now there are many beavers in their former range. In fact, they are so numerus that they are often a pest.

The Beaver

The beaver is a remarkable animal for many reasons. The most obvious thing about the beaver is its ability to construct a dam that will hold back water, thus creating a pond or lake.

So, what did the first beaver do if it did not already know everything it needed to know about building a dam? It could not *half way* build a dam. It would be much simpler to just find a stream that already had plenty of water. I lived on Cypress Creek and near Little Pigeon Creek for most of my life. Both flowed into the Ohio River. Since these creeks' water level never got very low, the beavers never had to build a dam to hold back the water. They cut trees; they stored hundreds of limbs under the water for a food cache during the winter, but they didn't need to build a dam and didn't. If, however, they needed to, they already knew how by instinct.

All of this *preprogrammed knowledge*, known as instinct, must be in an animal's brain when it is created in the womb or egg. Humans have been learning things for centuries, but not one scrap of new informational "knowledge" has been added to our brain. It would be nice if we knew how to read, write and do math as soon as we were born. It would be even better if we knew how to speak perfectly in the language our parents spoke and perhaps all the languages on earth. If we could pass on knowledge to the next generation by programing it into our DNA, then our offspring would instinctive know all the things that we do. If "evolution" can, by trial and error, program this knowledge into many lower forms of life, then we, as "intelligent beings" should be able to do it; right? We could program our DNA in the knowledge of how to drive a car, be a carpenter, cook, sew, play all the games that we enjoy and a host of other things. There would be need of schools. We could save a lot of money on education. However, we don't even know the basic things for survival unless we are taught.

The beaver already has all he needs for the work he does. He is a rodent with teeth that continuously grow his entire life. His teeth even have iron in them for extra strength for cutting down all the trees he fells. He knows not only *how* to build a dam, but *where* to construct it. He knows how to build a lodge, how to find a mate, court, mate with her, and help raise the young. He uses his tail not only to lean on for support as he is cutting down trees, but for building the dam and to slap the water as a warning to other beavers that danger is near.

If the beaver did not have everything he needs, including the knowledge of how to build a dam that will hold water, he could not survive at all. If he did not have all the instincts already preprogramed into his brain before he became a beaver, he could not even exist. Here is another example of the "omni-theory".

This is a baby groundhog or woodchuck, which is a rodent as is the beaver. The woodchuck is the second largest rodent in North America. The beaver is first. The capybara is the largest rodent in the world and is from South America.

Chapter 9

The Sand Grouse and the Pigeon

The sand grouse is a pigeon-sized bird that lives in deserts and dry arid regions of Africa. It is unique for several reasons, but the most astounding thing I believe is the way it brings water to its young. It must fly miles, and in some cases, many miles to find water. It, however, does not bring water back to its nestlings in its crop as many other birds do. It has "special" feathers on its breast. These feathers absorb and hold water. The sand grouse dunks its breast into the water until the feathers soak it up. It then flies miles back to its young and the offspring drink from their parent's breast feathers!

I would like to know how this "adaptation" could have evolved or why. If the ancestors of this bird fed their young some other way, how and why would they suddenly switch to another means of doing so? If they first fed their young with water in their mouth as do pigeons and many other birds, why would they change? This method works fine for most other birds. Even if the feathers suddenly changed on their breast to hold water, how would they know to dunk their breast so the water could be absorbed? If they even did this, why would the young suddenly change and drink water from the parent's breast instead of trying to get it from their mouth? The feather "modification," the young's instinct to drink differently, and the parent's instinct to soak their breast would all have to happen at the same moment or it would not work and they would die and the species would become extinct. All this is assuming you already have a bird that has survived for countless generations and then needs to change into another kind that feeds its young differently.

The common pigeon, like all doves and pigeons, drinks water by sucking it up. Most birds must tilt their heads back so the water will run down their throat. The pigeon is also very unique in the way it feeds its young. The majority of birds bring insects, fish, carrion, or some other food to their young. The pigeon, however, produces "milk" to feed theirs. It is called *pigeon milk* and it is produced much like a mammillary gland in mammals, only it is produced in its crop. When a baby pigeon, or dove as they are the same, is first hatched, it is blind, naked and helpless. It is also very small. *Both parents* produce this "milk" and feed the young from their crops. This milky substance is so rich that the young nearly double in size each day! In a week or so, the "milk" tapers off and they are fed seeds that the parents have in their crops.

I have raised pigeons and doves for many years and they are a fascinating hobby. The parents take turns incubating the eggs and covering the young, with the male sitting from about mid-morning to mid-afternoon. Then the female takes over. During courtship, they will lock beaks and "shudder" as if they are feeding their young. This shuddering they do when feeding their young, is a reflex action that causes them to regurgitate the "milk" or seeds into the mouths of their hatchlings. The offspring also have the instinct to put their beak into the mouth of their parents to get food.

In order for a pigeon to be a pigeon, it has to produce this milk or their offspring would not survive. Therefore, what did they do before they "evolved' into a pigeon?

A ruffed grouse from North America.

Chapter 10

Above are Buddy and Rambo. They were orphaned as tiny babies and I raised them. They never were caged, but were free to roam anywhere they wished to go. They were very playful and acted like pets growing up. Once they became older, however, they returned to the wild. They were on national television and I have a book written about them. There are also several videos of them playing together on YouTube.

Pets Gone Wild

It often it took centuries to get some of the breeds of domesticated birds or animals we have today. Out of all the thousands of creatures on earth there are but a handful that have been tamed or domesticated. A few are kept as pets only, such as dogs and cats. A few others are raised as pets, work animals, or even for the dual purpose of work and food. Dogs, horses, donkeys, camels, llamas, reindeer, water buffalo, oxen, and even elephants are used as work animals and the oxen, and reindeer are often used for food. Lastly, there are several that are used mainly for food: sheep, goats, pigs, chickens, ducks, geese, pigeons and guinea fowl.

The guinea fowl, which came from Africa, is the last bird to be domesticated. The Canada goose, peafowl, bobwhite quail and ring neck pheasant have been raised for many years in captivity and could someday be added to the list.

There is debate, however, as to some of the animals' ancestors. It is easier to identify where domesticated birds originated. The graylag goose of Europe is where most domestic geese came from. The wild mallard gave rise to all breeds of ducks, except the Muscovy duck. The rock dove or common pigeon is where all the breeds of pigeons came from. The red jungle fowl is where we got the domestic chicken.

With mammals, it is a little more difficult to know for certain where they came from. Most agree that cattle came from the now extinct wild auroch (the cattle seen on cave paintings in Europe) and the humped cattle of Asia, the Zebu.

Pigs are descendants of the wild boar that once ranged over all of Europe. Sheep and goats are believed to be from the wild sheep and goats that lived in the mountains of the Middle East. Horses, most believe, came from the tarpan, the wild horse that once lived in the forests of Europe and the same one depicted on cave paintings with the wild cattle. Others believe that domesticated horses may have also had Przewalski's horse of Mongolia as their ancestor.

The dog, most believe, came from the wolf and the house cat from the wild cat of northern Africa.

The tarpan, the wild European horse, became extinct in the late 1800s. Before they became extinct, some of them were breed to domestic horses. Once they disappeared, there were people that wanted to try to get the wild horse back. They did this by "back breeding." They took horses that looked like the wild tarpan and kept breeding them to get the appearance of the wild ancestor. The tarpans were light grey and had a dark dorsal stripe down their back. After many years of breeding, they did get a horse that looked like the tarpan and even released them back into the wild. By "back breeding", they also have cattle that look very much as did the wild auroch.

I agree with the auroch and zebu being the ancestors of cattle, but I do not agree that the tarpan or Przewalski's horse are the ancestors of the domestic horse. I am sure that the tarpan's blood is in many of our horses of today, but I think Przewalski's horse had little if any contribution to the bloodline. I have seen Przewalski's horse and have heard them "bray". If I was not looking at him, I would have thought that it was a donkey because its voice was not the whinny or neigh of a horse.

Przewalski's horse resembles the tame horses of Mongolia, with its stiff mane, but it is much larger and as I said, its voice is that of a burrow.

The main reason I do not believe that the tarpan is the sole ancestor of the domestic horse is because of the wild horses in America. In prehistoric times, there were wild horses in America, but for some "unknown" reason they became extinct. When the Spanish first brought horses to the New World, some of them began to escape and breed in the wild. After many generations, some of these horses began to get a dark dorsal stripe down their back just as the tarpan had. There were some, however, that also started showing up with stripes on their legs and even face! No known wild horse had stripes on their legs or face. Genes, however, hidden for centuries, began producing what had to be features that only their wild ancestors had. It is therefore my opinion that there was another wild horse, which was at least a great contributor to the domestic horse.

There is one other reason I believe this. The wild dromedary camel went extinct very rapidly. It disappeared from the deserts of Africa centuries ago. No one even knows how long they have been gone. The wild Bactrian camel, "two humped", is also nearly extinct in Mongolia. The reason being that they were so valuable that they were caught and domesticated. We know the tarpan went extinct, but if there was another horse that was even more desirable, it too would have gone extinct first. The Pére David's deer nearly became extinct before anyone even knew it existed and it had been around for thousands of years.

****

What happens, however, to pets or domesticated animals when they return to the wild? After going wild for only a few generations, most animals begin to look as their ancestors. Feral pigeons begin to turn blue-grey and have the white rump, as does the wild rock dove. Hogs begin to grow a longer snout, longer hair and lose the curl in their tail and they begin to look like the wild boar of Europe.

Feral dogs all over the world look very much alike. After a few generations, they begin to get a curled tail that they hold over their back. They also weigh about thirty pounds, and they do not look at all like a wolf. This is why I think that there could well have been another canine that is the ancestor of the dog for dogs can breed with wolves and even coyotes.

For many years, "scientists" said it took centuries to domesticate the dog from the wolf. Recent studies, however, has revealed that it only takes a few generations to "tame" wild animals. It was learned in Russia that foxes, which were raised for the fur trade, could be tamed in only ten years! By breeding the tamest ones over and over they began to change, not only in behavior, but also in appearance. The foxes began to get "floppy" ears, have white spots, or turn completely white. They also loved playing with people and would come when called. Several years ago, I had a relative that had a tame silver fox (a color phase of the red fox) that loved to be around people and would act just like a dog when it saw its master.

How and why would animals begin to look like their ancestors once they begin to live in the wild? Why would these once tame birds or animals that mate with others that were also once domesticated, begin to resemble their wild cousins? They could have mated with these same offspring if they would have been in captivity, so there must be something else going on. No one knows for sure, but I have an idea.

I believe it is because of the stress of living wild. Wild animals must not only find food, water and shelter, but they must be on constant lookout for danger. In captivity, all of their needs are provided for and they are not under the constant threat for survival.

Stress can cause all sorts of physical problems, disease, loss of weight, reproduction shutting down and even starvation. The stress of mating can cause some animals such as male elk to fight so much to protect his harem of cows that he will not eat and later dies during the harsh winter from the stress of his ordeal.

For many years, no one knew where the plagues of locusts came from. No one had ever seen any newly hatched locusts. Then, unexpectedly, millions of locusts would descend out of the sky and eat every green thing in sight. Only recently, it was discovered why no one had ever seen a baby locust. A newly hatched locust is green, not brown. It does not like being near another locust. However, in years when conditions are right, millions and millions of eggs hatch. The newly hatched locusts have nowhere to go and they are forced to be near one another. This stress triggers a hormone to be released in their body; when this happens, a metamorphosis takes place. They begin to turn brown, grow wings, and love to be near one another. "Nature" has designed this for a reason. When millions of locusts hatch, there will not be enough food for them, so they must move somewhere else to find it. In their "normal state", they could not hop far enough and all would soon die after eating their limited food supply. Therefore, they grow wings and fly many miles to find enough food to support themselves.

I believe that the stress of living wild may release certain hormones that cause gene mutations, which make it better for the survival of the species. We know that the lack of stress causes gene mutations in foxes, so it is no leap of faith that the reverse would also happen.

I believe in the not too distance future, when more study is done, that scientists will turn a page and finally get on the right tract about how life not only got here, but how and why nature, which was created by God, designed life to work as it does.

My cousin's tame silver fox.

Chapter 11

Is this your ancestor?

Primitive Man?

What about primitive man? Didn't we come from Neanderthals or some monkey, gorilla, or ape?

When I was a child in grammar school, in the early and mid-sixties, we studied "science." We were told then that just "ten-thousand years ago," our ancestors were primitive cave people! Moreover, "knowledgeable people" told us that in just the last ten-thousand years, primitive "ape-like humans" had "evolved" into modern man. As the years went by, "scientists" said that it took man much longer to "evolve."

Common sense would have told the ordinary person that a modern human being could not have changed from an ape-like creature into a man that looks like they do today in a few dozen generations. There are pictures carved in stone from thousands of years ago of ancient Egyptians that look just as they do today. Some stone figures were just four or five thousand years from what most "scientists" first said were people that had Neanderthal-like ancestors. It has been (and was in the 1960's) several thousand years since man was depicted on stonewalls that look just as they do today. This would mean that the "scientists" of just a few years ago wanted us to believe that man had changed so much in just two or three thousand years that he went from a Neanderthal to a modern man. If this was true, then men today should look quite unlike those of just two or three thousand years ago, but they do not; they look identical!

Over the years, fossils have been found that show there were several types of people on earth long ago. The Neanderthal had a larger brain than modern man, so why did the Cro-Magnon replace him? And what happened to the Cro-Magnon?

My most popular books are the seven in the series I titled *The Mammoth Slayers*, which is about the Neanderthals and the Cro-Magnons.

Today, there are several great apes: mountain gorillas, lowland gorillas, three subspecies of orangutans, and two species of chimpanzees. Then there are the gibbons, mandrills, baboons, and a host of smaller monkeys and primates. When anthropologists find a fossil of an ancient "human-like" skeleton, they say it is evidence that it was an ancestor of modern humans. We have no idea how many "human-like" primates there were long ago or *if* they were a "human-like" creature at all.

In the jungles and other places right now, there are primates that climb, some that run along the ground, and others that do both. It is very possible that there was a primate (or several) that walked upright, but was no more human than any monkey or ape of today.

Many point and say that a chimpanzee has almost the same genetic make-up as do humans. So does nearly every species on earth, even insects and invertebrates have much the same genetic code as we do. Most have over 90% of the DNA as we do.

There are only two possibilities: One is that there is no Supreme Being, no God, or there is. If He does not exist, then there is no rhyme or reason for anything in the universe, including us. If He does exist, then He had and still has a reason for His creation.

If you go to the Bible, for those that believe there is a God, He tells us that He made modern man. He says that He made him from the dust. We know that man is made of dust and returns to dust when he dies, just as God said in the beginning. Therefore, this is a fact. He also says that Eve is the "mother of all living." We know this is a genetic fact. Scientists have recently discovered what is commonly called the "Eve gene", which proves that all modern people came from one woman. Contrary to what many believe, nowhere in the Bible does it say that God did not have other humans or human-like creatures on earth. In fact, several Scriptures allude to the fact that He did.

In Genesis God said, "Let us make man in our image and after our likeness." This could very well mean that before modern man there were other humans that were not made in God's image, which had no chance for eternal life in His Kingdom.

Later in Genesis, God tells Adam and Eve to "go and replenish the earth." This sounds as if the earth was once full of life, but then life was destroyed and had to be renewed.

Even if you have a modern man, he is no different than any other mammal on earth except for a couple of small but unique differences. The only real difference is that he was made in the image of God and has a chance for eternal life as a child of God. Many do not understand that God is reproducing himself by adding humans to his family. I have written several books that explain more what the Bible says about this and other topics that few understand.

Chapter 12

A baby raccoon and kitten I raised together.

The following two chapters are partial excerpts from some of my other books. I have written over 80 titles and several of them are about the Bible, either end time prophecies, or on subjects many are interested in.

The first except is about evolution and it's near the end of the book *Christ: His Words, His Life* in the commentary.

The second excerpt is from a chapter titled *How Old is the Earth?* It's also from the same book. Both, however, are from another of my books, *Mysteries of the Bible*. In *Mysteries of the Bible*, which has over 54,000 words, I go into greater detail on the several other subjects and some mysteries revealed in the Bible. In addition, there is other things revealed by the history and traditions of God's people of ancient Israel. I wanted to include both excerpts, even though I have covered some of it already. I have more to say about the age of the earth, what happened in the Garden of Eden and several other topics in both of these other books.

Is the "Theory" of Evolution True?

Most take this as "Gospel" and it seems logical on the surface, but look deeper.

Darwin is the person that is attributed with the theory. A theory is a "possible" explanation of why or what happens to cause a certain event. It is a theory and stays a theory until it is proven beyond any doubt. Every "theory" in the scientific world has to be proven before it is accepted as fact, except one and that is evolution. This is because if this "theory" is not correct then the only other explanation is that God is the Creator of life. Since most do not want to "believe" this, *they have faith* that everything just happened on its own. It is more than ironic that many have their minds closed and are afraid to look deeper into other possibilities. This is not new. The religious leaders of Christ's time also had their minds closed. The Bible says that people will be "Ever learning but never able to come to the knowledge of the truth," II Timothy 3:7.

I have read that even Darwin had second thoughts of his own theory and said if everything was constantly changing, everything would be in a state of confusion.

"God is not the author of confusion, but of peace…" I Corinthians 14:33. You see this in nature everywhere. Every animal is "adapted" or designed for exactly what it does. Just stop and think about almost any bird or animal; how it lives and looks. Those that believe in evolution would have you believe that all this came by blind chance.

****

Take a **woodpecker** for example: It has a long, chisel-like beak for drilling into hard wood. At the end of its very long tongue, it has a hard tip with barbs on it to spear a grub or insect. Its tongue is so long that it splits in two at the back of its throat, and then goes under the skin around the back of its head, all the way to the top of its head. The tail feathers of a woodpecker are very stiff so that it can "prop" itself on the side of a tree. This is so it can be steady while it works to either drill a hole for a nest or to find food under the bark. Its skull also has a "cushion" in front, so that its brain is protected when it hammers the wood. Can you imagine the first bird trying to be a woodpecker and banging its head against a tree without this specialized equipment?

This is just one example. Every bird, animal, insect, or life form is so complex that there is no way it could have "blindly" evolved into the magnificent creatures they are today.

****

Evolution has no mind to think ahead and decide what it needs to do to create or change any lifeform. Even if it did know what was needed, it has no way to bring it about. Just as Christ said, "Who giving thought can add one inch to his statue."

Evolution has no eyes, so it cannot see. Evolution has no ears, so it cannot hear. Evolution has no brain so it cannot plan ahead. Evolution has no power to do anything because evolution is just a theory that came from the mind of men. Even men cannot create life from nothing.

I once heard a joke that I thought was pretty good. A scientist was talking with God one day and said, "I can create life, just give me some dirt and I'll show you."

"God replied and said, "You get your own dirt."

Today, men are so arrogant that they believe they are smarter than God. God created life from nothing. Before life or anything ever existed there had to be the laws of physics so that all of creation would obey those laws. Otherwise, nothing would or could exist. Laws cannot be seen, but all of nature obeys them.

****

Another remarkable bird (that recently became extinct) was the *huia*. They lived in New Zealand

and they were a wattlebird. They resembled a crow, but had small skin flaps (wattles) on their cheeks. What made this species so remarkable was that the male and female had totally different kinds of beaks. The male's beak was short and stout, like a crow, but the female's beak was long, slender, and curved downward in an arc! I would like to hear how the same species could have "evolved" a different beak for male and female. This defies all logic.

****

Now take the **bombardier beetle**. He has two separate chambers in his hind parts. Each chamber contains a different chemical that specialized glands produce. When he is in danger, he "shoots" these two chemicals together and they explode! This propels him away from the danger and this chemical mix is very hot and toxic. He can even aim this spray from a tiny tube-like structure that pivots. How could any creature slowly "evolve" by hit or miss chance and develop a gland that would produce the right chemical, in the correct formula, in the right place, at the right time, without a purpose for doing so in the first place? Then on top of this, it only works if he needs it. It is impossible this could develop without some supreme mind creating it!

****

The **flounder** is a fish that looks like any other when it first hatches from an egg. As it grows, however, it changes dramatically. One of its eyes "migrates" to the other side of its head and moves near the other. It then begins to lie on its side on the bottom of the seafloor. Those that believe in evolution say things evolved slowly over millions of years. Can you imagine the "first flounder" having its eye move somewhere else on its head and trying to lie on its side? For a flounder to be successful, it has to look like it is now and behave as it does. Anything "in-between" would not only be a disadvantage, it would be a disaster. I'm sure that a fish one day thought, "Hey, I think I will move one of my eyes to the other side of my head and then make my side look like my belly, so I can hide from predators on the seafloor!"

****

Those that "believe" in evolution say that birds evolved from dinosaurs. Can you imagine the first dinosaur that is going to change into a bird? Suddenly, one day, one hatches with feathers on his body. Why would he have them in the first place? What advantage would they be? In order to fly, he would have to have all of the correct feathers, in the right place and all at the same time. Feathers are very complicated. Each feather has a strong hollow shaft and very tiny "hooks" that zip the feather together. A bird also has to constantly preen them to keep them clean and working properly. Therefore, the reptile would also have to have a mouth "designed" to let him take care of the feathers. It would also have to have the knowledge imprinted into its DNA to do so.

Feathers cover a bird's body not only for flight but also for warmth. Each type of feather also has to be in the correct place on a bird's body and each feather has to be "programmed" in the genetic code to replace itself when molting or if one is pulled out.

A duck has feathers, but they would get soaking wet and the duck would freeze to death in winter if it did not have oil on its feathers. So, it "developed" an oil gland at the base of its tail so it can keep its feathers oiled and thus the water will "roll off its back?" Even if the duck had this oil gland, how would it know how to use it, unless its brain was "programmed" to do so? He would have to have *everything* that I mentioned and all at the same time or he would not be a duck.

A bird also would need hollow bones, so that it would be lighter. Even if a dinosaur had the "perfect body of a bird", he would not know how to fly. You can have a perfectly good airplane, but you cannot fly it unless you have someone that has been trained to do so. Even with a trained pilot, if something is wrong with the plane, if it is not "designed" correctly, it will crash and burn. I can guarantee that if you put feathers on a lizard, he will still crawl over rocks and under logs, just as he did before you put the feathers on him.

Now it is possible that God could have changed the dinosaurs into birds. When the Lord returns, He will change animals so the bear and lion will eat vegetation like an ox. He could have done this in the past. We have no idea. God has also designed life to change slightly in order for it to survive. Man has taken birds and animals and bred hundreds of different breeds, but they are still the same species. All races of people came from Adam and Eve. The same creature, if it is isolated, can change into different races, but you can never take a dog and over time change it into a cat.

Every creature has to have everything at the same time in order for it to be able to live as they are designed to live. If it is true that God took some of Satan's dominion from him and took away his "play things" (like dinosaurs), He could have redesigned them into birds. If you read about Satan as being beautiful once upon a time (Ezekiel 28:13-18) and his "wings" covered the throne of God, it is easy to see the contrast between the beauty of a glorious bird and the hideous look of a "terrible lizard." A beautiful bird in its glory and a lowly, ugly serpent in disgrace is a very good analogy.

There is also the possibility that dinosaurs did not die out until recently. Scientists thought that the coelacanth (a fish) died out before the dinosaurs even came on the earth, but in 1938, one was caught off the west coast of Africa. Since that time, other coelacanths have been found and of a different subspecies.

Just a few years ago, a T-Rex's leg bone was found. Upon cutting it in two, so it could be packed and shipped, 'soft material" was found inside the bone. It turned out that it was remnants of marrow and blood vessels. It is difficult for me to believe that a bone could have been in the earth for sixty million years and all of it was not turned to stone.

The Bible says that before the flood, the "sons of God" (angels) saw beautiful women and left "their own habitation," and married the women and they bore children unto them, Genesis 6:2. The Bible says these children became men of great renown. This could explain some of the ancient knowledge that still baffles people today. It also could explain how some of the ancient cities came to be built. Some rocks weighing nearly one thousand tons, which were cut with many angles, were moved up mighty mountains, and then lifted into place so precisely that they are nearly perfect to this day.

There is so much that we do not know or ever will, until the Lord returns. Apostle Paul said, "We see things through a dark glass, but then we will be face to face," I Corinthians 13:12.

Many people scoff at the Bible, but if they would have read and understood it, they would have known things centuries before they were "discovered." The Bible said that God "hung the earth on nothing," Job 26:7. It also talks about the "circle of the earth," Isaiah 40:22. This shows the earth is round, and hanging on nothing; that it is suspended in space.

I am not a scientist, but common sense tells you that if you take nothing and put it nowhere you will end up with nothing nowhere. Even if you have something and put it somewhere, it will not change, unless there are forces to change it. Only a creator God could create a universe.

God designed and created everything from "nothing." We can hardly change something once we have it, let alone starting from scratch. God said you could look at nature and see His creative genius. In Psalm 19:1, **"The heavens declare the glory of God; and the firmament shows His handiwork."** The Bible also says in Romans 1:20, "For the invisible things of Him from the creation of the world are clearly seen, being understood by the things that are made, even His Eternal Godhead; so that they are without excuse." Yes, on Judgment Day there will be no excuse to believe that God did not create everything we see.

Scientists are just now opening doors and seeing some of God's secrets in His design of the universe. Some of the things they are discovering sounds like spiritual explanations right out of the Bible of how God created and keeps in order a very complex universe.

I enjoy nature programs on television and it always amazes me how they explain how animals are able to do some of the things they do. In one sentence, they say, "it is a marvelous design." In the next sentence, they say it is an "amazing adaptation" or a "miracle of evolution." A design is something that has "forethought". Something cannot be designed unless there is a reason for it to be designed or created in the first place. Blind chance does not see the end result before it begins.

The "theory" of evolution is always stated as fact. The ones that say this also say that human beings are no more than any other animal, that we came to be here by blind chance and that there is no God, no Creator. Then people wonder why there is murder, rape, theft and other crimes. Why wouldn't there be if there is no God, no one to hold them accountable. Why not "eat drink and be merry, for tomorrow we will die." This is the same thing they said and did just before God destroyed the world during Noah's time. Christ also said that this same thing would be happening at the end of time just before He returns.

Yes, the lie of evolution, the "theory" of evolution is considered fact when it is ridiculous if looked at closely. Even a world-renowned atheist said it is not true.

Here is something I read in a magazine. The magazine was quoting from a book and from a man "long considered to be the world's best-known atheist." This man, Professor Anthony Flew, "shocked the world" because he believed that God existed. Not only that God existed, but also that God had to design life. He said this after studying DNA and "the complexity of the human cell." He said since the "beginning of his philosophical life" that he would follow the truth no matter where it leads him." It happened to lead him to see God's design in nature and therefore to see God himself.

Another *former* atheist, Lee Strobel, wrote a book called *The Case for the Creator*. He says the same thing. Even without the Bible, people are seeing God in His creation when they look at the mind-boggling complexity of life and the "programming" of living cells. Many world-renowned people are discovering and coming to the same conclusion that "no hypothesis has come close to explaining how information got into biological matter by natural means."

Yes, the DNA of all creatures is so complex that it is almost unbelievable. In the magazine, I mentioned above it says, "The six feet of DNA coiled inside every one of our body's one-hundred trillion cells contains a four-letter chemical alphabet that spells out precise instructions for all the proteins from which our bodies are made." To think that "blind chance" designed all the genes; genes that do an almost infinite variety of tasks, is difficult to grasp. Nevertheless, people do not want to see God in His creation and His design. They have "faith" in Satan's lie, the lie of evolution. Remember this: In order for there to be life, first there had to be order and God says He *is* a God of order.

Chapter 13

Photo courtesy of Peggy McDaniel

How Old is the Earth?

Many Christians think the earth is only six thousand years old, but look closely at what God says, not what you think He says.

In Genesis, 1:1, it says, "In the beginning God made the heaven and the earth." What were the first words? God made the heaven, and the earth. Therefore, the heaven and earth were here before the rest of the Scripture continues. "And the earth "was" **void** and **without "form,"** and **darkness** was on the face of the deep." The Hebrew word "was" can also mean, "became."

What does this mean? In Jeremiah, 4:23 it says, "I beheld the earth and lo it was **without form** and **void** and the heavens they had **no light**!" Without form means in chaos and void means empty.

Now this passage in Jeremiah is when hundreds of millions (or billions) of people are on the earth and it is during the Lord's wrath, during the Day of the Lord at the end of time.

The next verse in Genesis says, "And God said, 'Let there be light.'" Now if the heavens were already made, it means the sun was there along with the moon. If the earth and oceans were made before the sun, this would mean the oceans would be frozen solid.

If the sunlight was not reaching the earth's surface, there must have been a cloud of some kind obscuring the sun and He did say He separated the waters from the waters. This means He had to take the blanket of water (or perhaps a dust cloud along with the water from some catastrophe that struck the earth) away that covered the earth so the sun would shine.

Many times, in Scripture, the time of an event in one line of prophecy jumps for many years or centuries. The verse about the Lord's birth says He will be born in Bethlehem and the "government of the world will be on His shoulders." Now He still has not taken over the world as King of Kings and Lord of Lords. In this one sentence, there is a span of over two thousand years between the prophecy of Him being born and His return as King.

Look at what the Bible says in Psalm, 102:25-26; "Of old have you laid the foundation of the earth; and the heavens are the work of your hands. They will perish, but you shall endure; yes, all of them will wax old like a garment; as a vesture shall you change them, and they shall be changed." This means the earth and all the stars grow old and God changes them as we would a worn-out shirt. This seems to imply that He is old beyond counting.

In Psalm, 90:4, "For a thousand years in your sight are but as yesterday when it is past, and as a watch in the night."

If the heavens and earth are only six thousand years old and this is the beginning of all creation, this would mean that **God Almighty is but six or seven days old**! He would be **an infant**. That is **ridiculous!**

If a thousand years is as one day, then even if the Lord lived only one thousand years in *His* time, it would be 365,000,000 years to us. The Bible says that He is Alpha and Omega, the beginning and the end.

There is another Scripture 2 Peter, 3:8, which is a quote from Psalm, 90:4, but adds something else. It says, "One day is with the Lord as a thousand years, and a thousand years as one day."

Did you get that? It not only says that a thousand years to us is as one day to God, it also says that one day to us is as a thousand years to God. This means that God sees everything that happens in the smallest increments of time. He sees every "sparrow fall;" the firing of each and every spark plug in everyone's vehicle; the travel of each and every bullet fired from a gun and in ultra-slow-motion! One of our normal days seems like a thousand years to Him because He sees everything that happens down to the smallest detail. Since God is everywhere at the same time, He can see things in every way and all at the same time. We only see in three-dimensions and that's only because our brains take each eye's two-dimensional image and changes those two, two dimensional images into one that is in three-dimensions. We can only see up, down, in, out, east, west, north or south one direction at a time. God can see in every direction all at the same time, plus in every dimension that exists. He can do much more than our brains can even comprehend.

Now back to the discussion about the earth. The earth is just one average planet in our solar system, and our sun is just one average size star in our galaxy, which has countless, millions of suns. This is why the Bible says that the nations of the world are as "dust on a scale" and are "less than nothing!"

Many people try to put God in a small box so they can understand Him. He is beyond understanding in His glory, His majesty, His wisdom, and His ways.

I once gave a teaching about how Satan ruled the earth long ago. We know by what the Bible says that Satan has been given this world and he has power here. Now if this world has been his for who knows how long (only God knows) then his "mark" should be here on earth; right?

Look at the fossils of long ago, and what do you find? There was a time when nearly every creature on earth was a serpent! The "age of dinosaurs" had dinosaurs that ran on two feet; that crawled on their belly; that swam in the waters, and that flew in the air. The entire earth was "ruled" by serpents. Isn't it more than strange that in Revelation, God calls Satan that "Old Serpent?" In addition, it was a "serpent" in the Garden of Eden. The scarlet colored beast of Revelation 17:3 is a "dragon" which looks just like a dinosaur.

There is a Scripture in Psalm 74:13 which says, "You did divide the sea by your strength; you broke (or crushed) the head (seat of authority) of the "dragons" (or serpents) in the waters."

Moreover, in the Garden of Eden, God said that Satan would have to "crawl on his belly" and the woman's seed (Christ) would bruise his head. Most of the Garden of Eden story is symbolic of what happened and what will happen (The Tree of

88

Life was Christ and the Tree of Good and Evil was Satan). Satan, once called Lucifer, has always wanted to be like God. In Isaiah, 14:12, it says, "How are you fallen from heaven, O Lucifer, son of the morning. How are you cut down to the ground, which did weaken the nations. For you have said in your heart, 'I will ascend into heaven; I will exalt my throne above the stars of God. I will sit also upon the mount of the congregation, in the sides of the north. I will ascend above the heights of the clouds. I will be like the Most High.' Yet you shall be brought down to hell, to the sides of the pit. They that see you shall narrowly look upon you, and consider you saying, 'Is this the man that made the earth to tremble; that did shake the nations?'"

When Satan sinned in the Garden of Eden, God said his days were numbered. Also, in the book of Revelation in the 12th chapter, he is finally kicked out of heaven and brought down to the ground, or earth, for the last time.

Since he has been given this earth, and is the "prince and power of the air", I am sure he has done many things that God has not liked over the countless eons. His name Lucifer means, "Dawn Light" or "Bringer of Light" and he was once a mighty archangel. God crowned him with glory, beauty and splendor. However, pride entered his heart and he rebelled and wanted to be God himself. After this, he was called Satan, which means

Adversary. This explains why he has tried to destroy God's plan from the beginning.

If God has allowed man to "rule" this planet and ruin it by his greed and selfishness, I'm sure that in the past Satan did likewise. If God gave Satan the world to rule (and we know he has), what would he do with it? "Create", just like "a god" and what would he create? He would create serpents. They would also get bigger and bigger, and more terrifying with each generation. If you look at the fossil record of dinosaurs, it starts out with small animals and over time, they get bigger and more terrible until you have these giant serpents that walk on two legs; and have teeth like iron, and which kill and tear apart its prey. One of the last dinosaurs recorded was Tyrannosaurs Rex. It is somewhat odd that the name over the Lord's cross was in Latin and the Latin word for "King" is Rex. The name of Tyrannosaurs Rex means "King of the Tyrant lizards" or serpents.

Now if God has given man many chances to change and repent, I'm sure he also has done the same with Satan. God had to love him in the beginning and I'm also sure that if He loved him, He would "chastise" him. The Bible says that God, "Chastises those that He loves." Man has killed off species to extinction and has bred different animals to look completely different than they did before. Now he is doing experiments with gene splicing. Why wouldn't Satan do even more? He has much more knowledge than we will ever have. He has also been around for countless millennia to learn and practice what he wishes to do.

Most do not realize that he has great power. In the book of Job, he brings a tornado and kills Job's children. He brings all kinds of sickness and diseases also.

If you look at the fossil record, it shows one layer of sediment on top of another, just like layers of a cake. The layer above the other has very different animal fossils in them. It is as if God wiped the slate clean and started over. We have no idea how often the earth has gone through some catastrophic event in the distant past. The Bible speaks about the tectonic plates shifting rapidly, "Heal the breaches" (of the earth), Psalm, 60:2. In addition, "every island will be moved out of their places," as I mentioned before. Scientists have "theorized" that a giant meteor came from "heaven" and destroyed the dinosaurs! That sounds like something God would do; and if you look at how God has dealt with man, it is the same. He gave man a chance, but man became evil and then more evil until God nearly destroyed humanity by a great flood. Then He gave him another chance. It is very likely that He did the same with Satan.

Did Noah's flood really happen? Christ said, "As in the days of Noah, so shall also the coming of the Son of Man be," Matthew, 24:38. He reaffirmed that Noah lived and that a flood came.

Did the flood cover the entire earth? In prophecy, there is often a twofold fulfillment of an event. The first is much smaller than the latter. Adam (who was made by God) was the **first** man and all men came from him and he was made from **dust;** Christ was a man but became a "quickening **spirit**" when he was resurrected and was the first to be resurrected of the **many** brethren that sleep. This is similar to the Scripture that speaks about the **first harvest** in the spring, which is small. Then the **great harvest** in the fall, when the Lord returns.

In the prophecy of the kingdom of Babylon, it says that the kingdom "covered the entire earth." At the time, it did not, it only covered a small area of the entire world, but the "Babylonian system" would grow until it did cover the whole world by the time the Lord returns.

In the days of Noah, God destroyed man from the earth because of all the violence and sin. His only reason for the flood was to destroy man. The flood only needed to be large enough to destroy man from off the earth. He had Noah to save himself, his wife, his children and their wives.

God also had him to save many animals. He could have recreated the animals and had Noah and his family aboard a much smaller ark, but He didn't. If He had covered the entire earth with water, how did some of the flightless birds get to far away islands? Large flightless birds, called ratites, such as the ostrich, emu, rea, cassowary, kiwi and the extinct ones such as the dodo, moa and elephant bird would have had to be there already. These birds never have been able to fly because they have a flat breastbone and not a keel-type for flight muscles. Some of the flightless birds that do have keel-type breast bones could have flown there before they lost their ability to fly. Losing the ability to fly is not evolution, but God designed animals to change just like the different breeds so they can better survive. Of course, He could have taken these birds and animals to the islands Himself, but if He wanted to do that, He would not have had Noah build an ark in the first place.

He designed the entire universe to work on its own and He did this before the universe even began. His wisdom, and the laws He made, keep it going without fail. It also would be perfect except for the evil in the world. Someday that evil will be destroyed and then it *will* be perfect.

It is possible that the flood was a smaller type of destruction and the latter destruction at the end of this age will be worldwide as was the prophecy of Babylon and the "Abomination of Desolation" and many others.

We know that just before the dawn of "modern man" or right before or after the flood, there was a great worldwide extinction of animals. In America, we had mammoths, giant wild hogs, horses, camels, giant ground sloths, saber-toothed tigers, and a host of other animals and birds that have disappeared.

What could kill a saber-toothed tiger or a giant cave bear when much smaller predators survived? The large dire wolves died out, but not the smaller grey wolf. There were giant vultures with twenty-foot wingspans and several kinds of large bison, antelopes and others. What could have killed all of these animals when weaker, smaller animals lived? Some think it was "primitive man", but they were rare compared to now and why would they choose to kill the very large and dangerous, the fast and powerful, when they could kill the weaker species?

Another thought is if people in the days of Noah were as they are today; they could have killed off many animals. Many species of birds and animals are already extinct and others are on the way to extinction because of man's greed.

If you listen to what the Bible says about man it says, "Eve is the mother of all living." It does not say that she is the mother of all that have ever lived. We have no idea what happened before Adam and Eve came on the scene. God refers to the "harvest "of His saints like a crop. A farmer does not clear a field and plant only one crop. Some Native American tribes say that the world has been destroyed and replenished several times and I'm sure this could be true. In Genesis 1:28 "God said unto them, 'Be fruitful and multiply and **replenish** the earth.'" This sounds as if it was full of life at one time then destroyed and had to be replenished.

Genesis 2:4 "These are the **generations** of the heavens and of the earth when they were created in the "day" that the Lord made the earth and heavens.

Scientists say the universe is about thirteen and a half billion years old by the way it is drifting apart, and that could easily be correct. It could also mean that this is the first universe or the millionth. We have no idea what God has done in the past.

If you read what God says about man it says, "Let us create man in our image after our likeness." There is also the possibility there were other humans or human-like creatures that **were not in God's image**. In the past, God has been challenged by Satan to "prove" that God's way is better than his way; remember what happened to Job. I believe it is very possible that God became weary of Satan "messing up" God's creation and said He could make a creature that was made of dust that would choose good over evil and love Him. And now we are caught in the middle of that battle; the battle of the ages.

Chapter 14

    Above is a baby common snapping turtle. In only three weeks, he learned to "beg" for food. When he was hungry, he would come to the edge of the bowl and rear up on his hind legs wanting to be fed. He also recognized the food bowl when it was brought near and would come when he heard the bowl being tapped. If I sat my plate beside him on the coffee table when I was eating, he would also come near and rear up wanting me to give him something off my plate. You can also see he is very fat from all the food I fed him. Before the summer was over I released him near where he was found in a small ditch behind my house.

What's in the Mind of an Animal?

I wanted to write one short chapter about the minds of birds and animals. Long ago, most people that studied animal behavior believed that animals were just "dumb". As knowledge in this field has grown, many scientists have been surprised by the mental abilities of "lower forms of life." Many birds are very intelligent. Some jays can hide thousands of seeds all throughout the forest and remember where most are hidden. Crows, which are related to jays, can learn to make tools from sticks and use them to reach grubs inside of trees or logs. They can also learn several steps in acquiring food. Some have learned to pull up fishing line with their beaks and feet to obtain a fish or the bait that is on the hook. Others have learned how to place a nut, which they cannot crack, in automobile traffic, let the cars crack the nuts, and then wait until the traffic light stops the cars to retrieve their prize.

Sea otters use rocks to crack open shellfish. Chimps also use stone and stick tools. Not only do they use them, they often strip the leaves from the branches and break them to a length they want to suit their needs. When I was in school, I was told that making and using tools was what set humans above all other animals.

Animals can also communicate in ways that most never dreamed possible. Some chimps have even learned sign language. Others have learned how to push buttons on computers to tell people what they want. In addition, not only do primates have many facial expressions as we do, but every creature on earth has ways of communicating. Sometimes it is just a growl or threatening posture, but others can be very complex. Most male birds put on elaborate displays of courtship to attract a mate. Porpoises and whales sing or make clicking sounds to tell others of their kind "something." We are not yet smart enough to figure out what they are saying.

"Lower" forms of life, such as the octopus, can learn to remove a jar lid to reach food that is inside. Even goldfish, or other fish raised in captivity, will quickly learn to come to the surface to be fed.

Parrots can not only talk, but also studies have shown that at least some of them understand what words mean. Every dog owner knows that their pet understands many words that are spoken to them. I once had a black Lab that knew dozens of words. Besides knowing about twenty-five commands, she understood such things as, "Do you want to go outside?" "Get in the truck." Get in the boat," or "Where's the mouse?"

In the wild, many prey animals know when a predator is not hunting and will let the predator walk right by them. Sometimes it's the other way around. If you have watched nature shows, you have probably seen antelope walking right by a lion as it stands or lies nearby.

Not only do animals understand more than we think they do, they can often perceive our intentions. This is interesting because animals can often sense when humans are kind. One nature program you may have seen was when Jane Goodall was studying chimpanzees. One chimp was very mean and tried to kill the young of another female chimp. The terrified mother came to Jane with pleading eyes and you could see that she wanted Jane to help her.

I have heard stories of injured wild animals also coming to people for help. One story was of a red fox, which had a leg injury coming to a couple that lived in a mobile home out in the country. After the fox was better, it left, but later came back with another injured fox that also needed help.

Then there was a sick giant panda which came into a village for help. I guess, however, the most extraordinary thing I saw was a dog that tried to drag another dog that had been hit by a car from a freeway!

I have raised many kinds of domestic and wild animals and have studied nature all my life. During this time, I have had several experiences that seem very strange. On more than one occasion I have reached down and petted a young fence lizard as it sat sunning itself. It showed no fear of me.

Many years ago, I raised two orphaned raccoons called Buddy and Rambo. I named the one Rambo because he was so rambunctious. They were a handful, but darlings. I shot some video of them growing up and they were on the national television program Real TV back in December of 2000. I also wrote their story of how they came to be movie stars in a book titled *Buddy and Rambo: The Orphaned Raccoons*.

One night as I was feeding them, a strange wild raccoon came up with them to be fed. On another occasion, an opossum came on the porch as I was giving them cookies and also wanted to be fed. Tossing him a cookie, the opossum sat there on the porch and ate it. I suppose the wild animals could sense there was no danger by seeing others that had no fear of me.

Recently, I had another experience of a full-grown wild raccoon that came to the house and seemed not to have any fear of me. In just a few days, it would take food from my hand. I do not recommend anyone do this unless you have had a lot of experience with wild animals. Many wild animals carry rabies and I have seen a few. You must know how a wild animal is supposed to act and if they do not act normal, be careful because they could be ill.

Animals can also sense fear or can smell it. This is one reason why many people are sometimes attacked by bears, dogs or other aggressive animals.

Here is the most extraordinary thing that I myself have ever witnessed. Long ago, we had at least one grey fox coming to the house and eating cat food on the front porch. The food was for the two young raccoons I was raising. I saw the fox often with another nearby and they seemed tame compared to most foxes I had ever seen. After seeing them coming nearly every night for food, I wondered what one would do if I caught it. Therefore, after locking the chickens and other poultry in their house, I put a spring on the chicken coop door. I then tied a string to a stick, which held the door open and ran the string to a window in the house. After putting some scraps of meat on the ground, leading to inside the pen, I went in the house to wait.

Just before dark, a grey fox showed up, found the trail of meat and proceeded to eat as he walked right into the coop. As soon as the fox was inside the pen, I pulled the string and the door slammed shut behind the unsuspecting fox. Then, just as expected, the fox ran around the pen crashing into the wire trying to get out.

Rushing outside, I neared the pen expecting the fox to try even harder to get out, but to my surprise, he ran towards me, climbed the wire and sat on a tree limb I had put in the corner where my pigeons could perch. I had heard of grey foxes climbing trees but had never seen it myself. This, however, was not the most surprising thing it did.

101

Expecting the fox to go wild with fear as I approached, it instead sat there looking at me. "This is incredible," I thought. "Why doesn't it act afraid?" The wire of the pen was made of very small mesh so I knew the fox could not reach through it to bite me. Therefore, I thought I would try something. Reaching down and picking up a piece of meat the fox had missed, I held it up to the wire just in front of its nose. Then, to my utter amazement, the fox took it from my hand! I saw what was happening but I still could not believe it.

Calling my wife outside so she could be witness to this extraordinary event, she too fed the wild fox from her hand. If someone would have told me that they had done this I would not have believed them. It happened, I saw it, and I still have a hard time believing it myself.

There is a Scripture in Job, 5:23 that says, "For thou shalt be in league with the stones of the field: and *the beasts of the field shall be at peace with thee.*"

I hope this means that some of the animals can sense that I have God's Spirit living inside me and they know when I am no threat to them.

Above, is the wild raccoon eating cat food on our front porch. I called her "Stubby" because she had the tip of her tail missing.

Below, is another wild female raccoon and her young coming for a free handout.

Chapter 15

The above frog is a Wood Frog. Their habitat is moist woodlands where they hide under the leaflitter.

A Cry for Help?

I also have this story also in my books *Barnestorming the Outdoors: Revised edition* and *Do Pets go to Heaven?*

A Cry for Help is a little different kind of story and one I did not originally include in this book. However, since it is about wildlife and how evolution could not possibly account for the marvels in the natural world, I thought it should be included. This story does not give an insight into the physical impossibility of evolution but a spiritual one, and I thought some might enjoy it.

****

One day, while in my backyard, I heard a strange noise. It was coming from near the creek a few yards from my house. At the time, I lived on Cypress Creek, which is near the Ohio River, in Warrick County, in Southern Indiana. The creek was at the bottom of a hill behind my house, and I had cleared and mowed all the way to the water, so I would have a good place to fish.

As I stood there listening, I did not know what could be making the sound. It wasn't a bird or an insect, and it didn't sound like any animal I had ever heard before. The sound was a high-pitched *cry*. Being interested in nature since childhood, I was curious as to what was making the odd sound, so I went to investigate.

Nearing the creek, I followed the sound and soon saw something move in the short grass near the water's edge. There, a few steps away, was a crayfish tunnel, which was about eight to ten feet from the edge of the water. As I peered through the short grass at the entrance of the hole, I saw the source of the noise. A small leopard frog was half in the hole and half out; but why was he making the crying sounds? Suddenly he moved, and I saw the reason. He was being held tightly in the jaws of a garter snake. The snake was in the crayfish tunnel with his head just visible, and he had the frog's hind legs in his mouth, trying to swallow him.

Looking down at the poor frog, I couldn't help but have compassion on it. It would be a terrible way to die, to be slowly swallowed alive and then to succumb to the burning acid in the darkness of the snake's belly.

The little frog continued to cry, as I searched for a stick.

Returning to the crayfish's hole, I held the snake's head with the stick and freed the frog. I am sure that the snake was disappointed, but I'm also sure the frog was greatly relieved, as he hopped towards the water and dove under the surface to the safety of the bottom.

After the incident, I began to reflect on it. Why did the frog cry out? Was it fear? Was it pain? Was it a cry for help?

I have been on earth for nearly seventy-three years as I update this book in November of 2023. I have spent countless hours in the woods and along streams and I have never heard a frog *cry* before. As a child, I loved hunting bullfrogs. I killed hundreds; cleaned them, and fried their legs. However, all the times they were killed, *not once* did one cry out. In addition, in biology class during high school, I saw many frogs killed by a slow painful insertion of a pin to the brain, and not once did one make a sound.

So why did this one cry out? It was not that painful, for he was just being held by the snake, and even if it was, they don't cry out if hurt. It could have been fear; but the countless frogs that I've seen die slowly must have known they were dying and never cried out. Was it then a cry for help? If so, why would a frog cry for help? No other frogs would or could come and rescue it. Birds give a warning cry when they see a snake, and other birds of many species will come and try to drive the snake away. The young of many birds and animals cry for their mother's help when afraid or in danger. Mother animals will attack or try to lead a predator away. Some birds, such as a killdeer, even "pretend" to be injured to lead an animal away from its young. Often, however, when a bird or animal does cry out, it will only bring predators. Upon hearing a bird or animal in distress, a predator will think they can have an easy meal. Most kinds of frogs, on the other hand, usually lay their eggs in water and never see their young.

After thinking on it for a while, I came to the conclusion that *it was a cry for help*; not for its mother; not for others of its kind; but it was *a cry for help from God.*

I came to this conclusion for several reasons. One was why would a frog or any creature cry for help when there is none? God will not reach down and save an animal that is the food of another. The reason is in the Bible. In Romans 8 and beginning with verse 19: *"For the earnest expectation of the creature waits for the manifestation of the sons of God. For the creature was made subject to vanity, not willingly, but by reason of Him who hath subjected the same in hope. Because **the creature itself also shall be delivered from the bondage of corruption** into the glorious liberty of the children of God. For we know that the **whole creation groans** and travails **in pain** together until now."*

If you wish to learn more about this, I have written a book titled *Do Pets go to Heaven?*

All of nature and its creatures cry to be delivered by God from death and destruction. Moreover, since *we are the sons of God*, we have the power to intervene and rescue a helpless creature. The Bible tells us that those that are His are called the *sons of God* and it says this in John, 1:12, Romans, 8:14, and 1 John, 3:1-2. Of course, the frog did not know that a human, who is made in the image of God, would deliver him; but his cry *was* heard. Who knows how many millions of frogs have been eaten by snakes since the dawn of time and not one was saved; so, their cry for help would seem to be in vain, but it wasn't. In Job, 38:41 the raven's *"young ones cry unto God."* When God sets up His kingdom on earth, all the cries for help from every creature, including us, will be heard, and *we shall **all** be delivered.* Then it will come to pass what was said in Isaiah, 11: 6-9, *"The wolf also shall dwell with the lamb, and the leopard shall lie down with the kid; and the calf and the young lion and the fatling together; and a little child shall lead them. And the cow and the bear shall feed; their young ones shall lie down together; and the lion shall eat straw like the ox. And the sucking child shall play on the hole of the asp. They shall not hurt or destroy in all My holy mountain; for the earth shall be full of the knowledge of the Lord, as the waters cover the sea.* I am looking forward to that day.

Chapter 16

These are ducks and geese running for *joy* when they are released from their pen to feed in the yard.

Do Animals Feel Emotions?

I did not originally have this chapter in the book, but I thought it needed to be added. I had it first in my book *Do Pets go to Heaven*?

All of us that have or have had pets, have raised farm animals, seen animals in the wild or on television, know that animals have a range of emotional behavior. This photo above is an example of the joy animals feel when they are happy. The ducks and geese in the photo above were just let out of their pen. I knew they would act this way because I had always let them out each day to have some freedom and eat grass in the yard. I had the camera ready and snapped several pictures. I had to keep them penned up for their own good because of all the predators that lived in the nearby forest.

Every day that I went to let them out, they would be crowding near the gate knowing what was about to happen. Then, as soon as the gate was open, they would run across the yard and beat their wings trying to get off the ground. The geese would honk and look at one another as if they were telling the others how good it felt to be free.

Anyone that has ever had a dog knows how happy they are to see you after you've been a way awhile and come back home. My dog, Princess, used to wait by the window when it was time for the school bus to arrive in the afternoon. I do not know how she knew it was time for it, but she did. About five minutes before it was to arrive, she would sit there and wait. Then, when she heard the brakes of the bus being applied to stop, her tail would begin to wag. Peeking out the window, she would watch the bus slow down, stop, and my two boys get off. She would then run to the kitchen door and wait until they came in. After greeting them, she would walk away and go back to her normal behavior. Once, when my father came for a visit, he happened to notice that Princess' water bowl was nearly empty. Therefore, he went to the kitchen sink, filled her bowl with water, and gave it to her. All the time he did this he was talking to her saying things like, "The poor dog is out of water and no one will get her any." She wagged her tail in appreciation, then walked over and took a drink from her bowl. After that day, every time my father would come for a visit, she would meet him at the door. And as soon as she saw that it was him, she would go get her water bowl and carry it in her mouth, with water sloshing all over the floor, and try to give it to him. She wanted him to know that she remembered what he had done.

I remember reading a story once of a dog that loved his master so much, that when the old man died, the dog went and lay on top of the grave. Here he stayed, only leaving for short periods to eat. The dog stayed there on that grave for several years until he, too, died. People that knew about it were so impressed by the dog's loyalty that they buried the dog beside his master.

When I had pygmy goats, they would often show joy in the evening as the sun went down. It would be cooler then and they would run, jump, kick up their heels and play with one another. They would jump on something, such as a stump, and play king of the hill and try to butt one another off. You could easily see that they were feeling joy and happiness.

Animals also have fear. We see this all the time when they run from us or a predator. God had to put this fear in them for their own survival. They also feel anger. Just give two strange dogs a bone and see what happens. Anger is there to keep other males from mating with the dominant male's females. It is also there to help assure that the animal will have enough to eat.

In the world now it is literally dog eat dog. Many species of birds and animals seem cruel in the way they behave. Often, if they have too many young to care for, they will let some of them die by starvation or even kill them. This is to ensure that the others will live. Even nestlings will often kill one another if there is not enough food. House sparrows and European starlings were brought here to America and released. If they can evict woodpeckers or purple martins from their nests, they will. They will even toss out the young to let them die. The same goes for parasitic birds such as the European cuckoo or the cowbird in America. In the future, all this will change and animals will be at peace with one another. I explain this in several of my books about the Bible and God's coming kingdom.

My pygmy goats.

Chapter 17

The gorgeous Lady Amherst pheasant. This is one I raised.

What do Scientists Say?

Most people of course believe in evolution. Even many that proclaim to be followers of Christ believe in it. They have been deceived into believing a lie. There are a growing number of scientists, however, that do not believe evolution is possible and believe in creation.

I got online and looked at dozens of scientists that say that life could not have evolved. Not only scientists, but also many doctors believe that the "miracle of life" could not have evolved on its own.

According to a recent survey, 40 percent of Americans do not believe in evolution. This means more are not sure. Those that rule out the possibility of creation therefore must be the minority.

One person did a review of this book and said that they did not want to hear what the Bible or God said about creation, they just wanted hard evidence from other sources. (I'm paraphrasing their comments).

I have a large book on birds, which was published in 2007 by the Audubon Society. It is a beautiful book with colored photos of hundreds of spectacular birds. They, like many others, state evolution as fact. However, they admit there are a lot of problems in "tracing the path of evolution" with many species. One group of birds leave them with many unanswered and "unsolved questions" as they put it. The birds are the ratites. Ratites are ostriches, rheas, emus, cassowaries, kiwis and tinamous, along with some extinct species, such as the giant moa and the elephant bird.

Ratites have no keel on their sternum. This is the breast bone, where in other birds the muscles are attached for flight. Since they do not fly, they do not need a keel. For many years the evolutionists took for granted that they all had the same ancestor. They believed this ancestor gave rise to all of those ratites living today or that that have recently gone extinct. They also believed this "ancestor" lived millions of years ago on what many call the ancient continent of Gondwana or Pangea. This was believed to be the giant land mass that broke up and drifted apart, which became the continents of today.

Recent DNA evidence, however, tells a different story. It seems that the ratites did not have an ancestor that gave rise to all of them but "that they diverged much more recently, which throws this theory into doubt." They go on to admit that there are "similar puzzles with several other groups" of birds. If they did not have one ancestor that gave rise to all the ratites when they all lived on Pangea, then how did they get to different continents?

The helmeted Guinea fowl of Africa is not classified with pheasants, yet they have crossed with peacocks, which are a type of pheasant that live in India. New world quail will not hybridize with old world quail and neither will wood ducks cross with Mandarin ducks, which look nearly indicial except for plumage. There are so many unanswered questions and evolution does not have an answer.

If evolution was true, then this means there is no God and everything just came about on its own with no rhyme or reason. If there is no God, then life has no meaning except for the brief period we exist. If on the other hand, God did create the universe and life, then He is the one we need to go to for answers.

Christ said in the Gospels, in Matthew 11 and Luke 18, that many things are revealed to those with child-like faith and are hidden from the wise.

Apostle Paul said in 2 Corinthians that the Gospel (the good news) is hidden from the world because Satan has blinded those that do not believe.

As I said in an earlier chapter, those that believe in evolution must have "faith" that what they believe is true. The same goes for those that reject evolution and believe only the mind of God could create such a universe and life in it. They see the indisputable proof that only God could have created such a world with all of its laws and diversity.

If we were to come across a space ship and looked inside to see how complicated it is, I think only a fool would believe that it just built itself. What is more amazing is that the universe is filled with trillions of "space ships" (worlds, planets, suns, moons, galaxies, and other heavenly bodies.) These worlds are much more complicated than any man-made or alien space craft, let alone the miracle of life. The simplest life form is much more complex and complicated than any space ship.

Romans 1:20-22 says, "For the invisible things of God from the creation of the world are clearly seen, being understood by the things that are made, even His eternal power and Godhead; so that people are without excuse. Because when they knew God, they did not glorify Him as God, neither were they thankful; but became vain in their imaginations, and their foolish heart was darkened. [And] professing themselves to be wise, they became fools."

There is another Scripture that shines some light on what was already taking place two thousand years ago. It is a letter from Apostille Paul to Timothy: 1Timothy 6:20, "Timothy, keep that which is committed to your trust, avoiding profane *and* vain babblings, and oppositions of ***science falsely so called***, which some professing have erred concerning the faith."

"So-called science" or "false science" is what Paul warned Timothy about, which denies the overwhelming evidence of creation by a loving God, and instead, embraces "false evidence" of why the world is the way it is. Belief in what these "so-called false scientists" say have caused many to lose their faith in God.

Yes, I would rather put my faith in what God says than in what man says, whether it is a scientist or any other scholar. We will not stand before a man on Judgment Day to give account of our life, but before God.

Chapter 18

Another of my birds, the spectacular Golden Pheasant.

The "Truth":
According to Evolutionists

Recently, I happened to catch an old episode of the Johnny Carson show. It was originally aired on May 20, 1977, and one of the guests that night was Carl Sagan. Carl Sagan, for those that are too young to remember, was a "scientist" who was an "expert" in the study of outer space. Mr. Sagan was often on the show and even had television programs of his own. He was world renowned for his expertise as a scientist. He was the professor of astronomy and a space scientist at Cornell University and director of the laboratory for planetary studies. He was an author of several books, and often gave speeches and lectures to other "knowledgeable people". He was on the show that night to promote his new book, *The Dragons of Eden: Speculations on the evolution of human intelligence*.

Carl Sagan was (he is deceased now) supposedly one of the brilliant minds of our time. I watched and listened carefully and even recorded the program so I could quote him exactly. I had seen the program a few months earlier, but didn't have it recorded. I wanted to use his own words to show how those that believe the lie of evolution will say almost anything to perpetuate their beliefs. You will see how ludicrous, ridiculous and right down nonsensical were some of the things he said when it came to how intelligence "evolved."

Mr. Sagan was trying to explain how humans became humans. How we are more intelligent than other forms of life and how information could be passed on from one generation to another.

He said, "We have information stored outside of our bodies."

He explained that we can pass on information by writing it down, telling others by verbal communication, and then the next generation can use that information. This if true and a book that was written even thousands of years ago can be read just as if it was written yesterday. We now have computers in which to store information and pass that knowledge onto the next generation. This book you are reading has information that can be passed on to others.

Mr. Sagan was telling about how early life forms only used "information stored in their genes", which is known as instincts, and used that information to survive. He then went on to explain what is *supposed to have happened* that caused intelligence to make a *giant leap* forward.

Here are his exact words: "For most of the history of life on this planet, the organisms had almost all of the information they had to deal with in their genes; heredity information, instincts. Then about *a hundred million years ago*, maybe a little more than that, *there came to be a reptile* that for the first time in the history of life, that had more information in its brain than its genes. And that was a major step, symbolically, in the evolutionary life on this planet."

If a three-year-old child said this, they would be thought of as speaking foolishness. "A *reptile* suddenly has "more information in its brain than in its genes." What is it going to do with this information? The other reptiles around this reptilian Einstein are so dumb and stupid that he can't pass that information on to them because they are not as special as he is. He cannot talk or write down the information. Even if he could, the others cannot read or speak. Also, why did it happen one hundred million years ago? That number just seems to pulled out of thin air. Scientists are not supposed to state something as fact, unless it can be proven. What happened to that reptile? The answer is, he died along with all the others because according to all those that believe in evolution, the dinosaurs died out several million years later. If that is the case, then the "information" was lost even if it ever existed, which it didn't.

No, the dinosaurs did not record what happened to themselves. I'm certain we will never find a stone tablet that some T Rex used to chisel his thoughts or tell the history of how his fellow reptiles were facing extinction. For one thing, his arms were too short to use a hammer and chisel. For another, the hammer and chisel hadn't been invented yet.

I'm being a little sarcastic and facetious, but I want to show how stupid some of these so-called scientists are. And Carl Sagan was supposed to be one of the brightest. It has been a hundred million years since that "reptile" first had more information in his brain than in his genes, so what are replies doing today? Are any in collage? What inventions have they made? Have they found any cures for diseases? Why didn't they see their own extinction coming and prevent it?

I have the answer. Reptiles today are the same as they were a hundred million years ago. In fact, they have gone somewhat downhill. Once upon a time, many of them walked on two legs, now they all crawl on the bellies. Where have I heard that before? Yes, I've heard that somewhere else. I believe it was said in the Garden of Eden. Oh, wait, that is the title of Mr. Sagan's book, *The Dragons of Eden*. But Carl Sagan was an atheist. How could he use something the Bible says to make money? He did not believe in God. Everything in the universe just came from nothing on its own and arranged itself in the mindboggling complexity as we see today. No, I do not think he was smarter than Albert Einstein and Einstein said there had to be a God because the universe was in perfect order and it could not have happened without someone planning it.

It is more than ironic to me that Mr. Sagan said a "reptile" a "serpent," a "dragon" was **the one** that suddenly had more information than he needed and wanted to pass it on. "You shall not surely die" was what the "reptile" said to Eve, which was the first lie. "He (the serpent, which was symbolic of Satan) is the father of lies" and continues to spread his lies, but now through men and women, many of which call themselves "scientists." There is nothing wrong with knowledge, or scientific study if it is indeed true.

During the interview, Johnny asked Mr. Sagan this: "Do you think if something happened to humans. Suppose tomorrow; in theory, if all human beings disappeared from the earth and it was left just to the birds, the fish, the reptiles and the animals; you think they would evolve eventually into speaking like we are, or has that evolutionary time; have we passed that?"

Carl Sagan answered, "I think it is very likely…" He goes on to say, "It's an interesting question. Which organism would replace us if we wiped ourselves out? An old professor of mine, H. J. Muller said he thought it was between *raccoons and bears*. They're both very clever and can do different things. But my feeling is that the great apes: chimps, gorillas are so close to us already that they have a big head start."

What's interesting to me is that one of Carl Sagan's professors said that if humans died out raccoons or bears would eventually evolve into humans. Here, in my opinion, is a fool teaching a fool. Bears and raccoons are supposed to have been here long before humans even stood upright. They are still the same and have not changed. Sagan said apes would replace humans and be able to talk. This would make some entertaining movies, which have already been made, and I enjoyed the many Planet of the Apes films, but that is fiction! Monkeys and apes, according to evolutionists, have been here long before man, so why haven't they "evolved" into walking upright, speaking and writing. If they had, they would have been far more successful and many would not be facing extinction today. They have been here millions of years longer than we have, (according to most scientist) yet they are the same as they were when we supposedly broke off from their evolutionary tree and became humans.

There was also something else that Carl Sagan said that caught my attention. He said "We are in very perilous times." He was referring to the nuclear age where man can destroy all life from the earth. That caught my attention because his words (I'm sure unknown to him) was exactly what Apostle Paul said in the second book of Timothy about two thousand years ago. It is in II Timothy 3:1: "This know also, that in the last days perilous times shall come."

Why did Carl Sagan say we are in perilous times? Because humans have passed on knowledge and information to where we now have the capability to destroy all life from the planet. This was also said by Christ, if Mr. Sagan would have cared to look. "Unless the time shall be shortened no flesh would be saved," Mathew 24.

Christ said the same thing, but two thousand years ago. Not only did He say it could happen, He said it *would happen*!

Long before Christ said this, the prophet Daniel was told by an angel sent from God that near the end of time, "Men shall travel all over the world and knowledge shall be increased."

Apostle Paul also said something that sheds light on the days in which we are living. He said those that think they are smart will be "ever learning, but never able to come to the knowledge of the truth," II Timothy 3:7.

If Carl Sagan or any person really wanted to understand the universe, he should have read what **The Creator** of the universe has said.

Those that do not believe in God must have something to believe in to take His place. Most believe in man and man's knowledge. You can see where that has taken us. We were given intelligence and yes, we have invented many wonderful things, but the heart of man is the same.

Mr. Sagan said this before the interview was over. He was speaking about the possibility of humans destroying themselves from this planet. He said, "I hope it won't happen. The way to guarantee it doesn't happen is by using the intelligence that *nature* has already given us."

It wasn't "nature" that gave us our mind and the intelligence it contains, it was our Creator, God. Our minds, however, have also been poisoned by "the adversary" way back in the beginning. That knowledge is the beginning of wisdom. Mr. Sagan was right about "the dragon of Eden," he just didn't understand the rest of the story. He believed the lie of the dragon, the lie of evolution.

My dog, Princess, in 1985.

Epilogue

Entire books have been written contradicting the "theory of evolution" and by using just one species of animal. I could, however, give a list of dozens or hundreds of birds and animals that have extraordinary abilities that dispute the absurdity that such abilities evolved. The hummingbirds whose wings move so fast that most cameras cannot even photograph them without it looking like a blur; whose heart beats hundreds of times a minute and are the smallest of all birds. The giraffe, whose heart has to be huge to be able to pump blood up its long neck; the neck that has several valves to regulate the blood flow, so it will not pass out when it lowers it head to drink.

And what about the fairy tern that lays its single round egg on a bare limb. Here it sits and hatches the young that also must balance itself on a small limb without a nest. Wouldn't it survive much easier in a nest or on the ground as do most birds?

I could talk about the kangaroo and other marsupials whose young are so tiny and premature that they have no hind legs formed yet, but are able to climb from the womb up into the mother's pouch and attach themselves to a nipple.

I watched a nature program just a while back and what they said was so ludicrous that I couldn't believe they said it. They said the kangaroo "developed a pouch from a loose fold of skin on their belly." The skin then slowly, over time, became larger and made a pouch.

So, my questions are, "Did the nipples the baby joeys needed to survive suddenly grow in a different place on the belly? Where were the nipples before? How did the premature joey know where the nipples moved to when it had to crawl

129

out of the womb and find the undeveloped pouch? How did they survived for millions of years before the mother kangaroo "decided" to change what worked and try something different?

It would take a giant leap of faith to believe something so ridiculous, so asinine, so stupid that it boggles the mind.

The elephant is another astounding creature, which has a trunk that is controlled by thousands of muscles. Their trunks also have amazing flexibility, which is so great that they can pluck one blade of grass from the ground or lift a huge log. No other creature on earth can do anything close to this, and they do it with an elongated nose.

Then, there are whales that communicate over hundreds of miles in the vast oceans. What did they do before they could "talk" to one another? How could they find one another to mate if their communication slowly evolved? They couldn't have, and they would have died out.

What about all the birds that migrate all over the earth and return to the same nest year after year? How did the bat fly without hitting a tree or some other obstacle before it developed echolocation? It had to have the echolocation before it could fly and hunt for food. It also had to be able to fly at the same time it had echolocation. If it had one or the other, it would do the bat no good and it could not survive. It could not slowly "evolve" echolocation and flight at the same time.

It had to be a bat with all its super abilities at the same time.

I would love to hear the explanation of why a spider would leave its "normal web" and begin to use one to throw over its prey as a fisherman casts his net. In addition, how and why would a frog lay its eggs and the male put them in "pockets" on his back to hatch? There is another frog that even goes further. He takes the tadpoles up a tree and puts them in a hollow that has water! Why on earth would a creature make it more difficult for itself to survive?

Then there is one other frog that does something so incredible that when it was discovered zoologists said it was *"impossible."* It has a way of hatching and taking care of the tadpoles that is so unbelievable that even after it was discovered and photographic evidence was shown, no one believed it.

I myself did not know about this fog until I was finishing this book, but since it is so astonishing, I had to include it. The frog was only discovered in Australia 1972. Two years later, as it was being studied, its amazing reproductive secret was revealed. It is a gastric brooding frog, and there is (or was) two species of it, for shortly after their discovery they became extinct.

What makes this frog incredible and shoots down the "theory" of evolution is this: The female, after laying her 20 to 25 eggs and having them fertilized by the male, swallows them! When they enter her stomach where they would normally be digested like any other food, her stomach stops producing acid! After her stomach acid is shut off, the eggs begin growing. Then, even after they hatch, they stay in her stomach and develop there for six full weeks. All the time they are developing, she cannot eat. This is incredible enough, but what's more, is that because her stomach swells so much with the developing tadpoles, her lungs collapse! Amazingly, she does not die because she can no longer use her lungs to breathe; she begins to get her oxygen through her skin!

It is funny to me, that scientists, when they first heard this, would say this was "impossible," because the Bible says otherwise. Matthew 19:26 "But Christ beheld them, and said unto them, 'With men this is impossible; but with God *all things* are possible.'"

I believe that as our knowledge has increased (as predicted in Daniel 12:4) and many secrets about our world have been uncovered, God has shown us more incredible things that He has created. In ancient days, life seemed simple and it was easy for people to believe in many gods. Now it seems that few feel they need to believe in any god, let alone the Creator of the universe. However, with the increased knowledge of today, and the "impossible" things that He has designed, people will be without excuse for not believing that He has done it.

Yes, each and every creature on earth is *designed* to do what it does to survive in a sometimes-hostile environment. It is designed to find a mate, raise its young, hide from danger or fight when it needs to.

Some who believe in God think that God directed evolution. The planets, stars, and other heavenly bodies could change slowly over eons of time, but a living organism would have to be complete in order to function as it was meant to. Even the earth and stars had to have a "Master Mind" behind it. Each step of the way would have to have been known before it began, just as if we would build an airplane or some other complicated machine. The entire universe would have to have a plan and the laws that govern it would have to have been in place before it began, otherwise it would not work. Albert Einstein was one of the greatest minds of all time and he knew everything could not have unfolded by "a row of the dice." He could see order in the universe and knew it was ruled by laws. The Bible says that God is not the author of confusion but of order. There is order in the universe, and there is order in the way all creation is made and in the way it functions.

There is only one reason that there are so many extraordinary life forms on earth. It is because God designed them for His own pleasure. He wanted to make a countless variety of life. He loves life and said in His word *"He made the earth to be inhabited"*, Isaiah, 45:18. He wanted to use *His knowledge in designing* almost unbelievable life forms and make them do extraordinary things. He also made them for us because we were made in His image. We, like Him, can take pleasure in His creation. No other creature on earth sees and appreciates all the things that God has made.

I could write about every creature that has ever lived and how it was designed perfectly for the life it leads, but that would not matter if someone does not want to believe. If they want to believe and have faith in evolution, it will be a waste of my time and effort and their time reading what I have written. For those that believe in evolution will say creation happened by accident; that it unfolded by blind chance. They give glory and praise to chance or to the creature itself, but not to the One that created it. I quoted the Scripture before but I will quote it once more. Romans, 1:20 says, *"For the invisible things of Him from the creation of the world are clearly seen, being understood by the things that are made, even His eternal power and Godhead, so **they are without excuse.**"* Here is what the Bible says about those that do not believe that God created all things and that He is just a myth. Verse 22 says, *"Professing themselves to be wise, they become fools."* Then in verse 25 it says, *"Who changed **the truth** of God **into a lie,** and*

worshipped and served he creature *more than the* ***Creator***…*"*

So, who will be right, the evolutionists that believe life came about on its own or those that believe God created it? Time will tell.

I thank you and hope you enjoyed reading this book. If you have, please tell others about it and my other work. I will leave you with one of my many "proverbs." It shows the greatness, grandeur, and brilliance of our Creator and all the splendor He has created by His wisdom.

****

"The earth is but a grain of sand on the beach where God walks." This is one of the "Lost Proverbs" from my book titled *The Book of WISDOM (Words Instructing Spiritual Direction Of Man).*

About the Author

Kenneth Edward Barnes has been called, "*A modern day Mark Twain*" by a local newspaper reporter for the first book he wrote titled *Life Along Little Pigeon Creek*. "*He shows a Twain sense of humor in conversation and in his writing. He writes in the 'down to earth' style that Twain used to capture the heart of America.*"

He was born on April 4, 1951, along the banks of Little Pigeon Creek in the southern tip of Indiana, downstream from where Abraham Lincoln grew up. As a child, he loved fishing from the muddy banks of the creek and roaming in the nearby woods. He never missed an opportunity to be in the outdoors where he could see all of God's creation.

Ken is a nationally published writer, poet, and the author of over one hundred books. Some of his most popular ones are: *The Mammoth Slayers; A Cabin in the Woods; Mysteries of the Bible; Madam President; Life Along Little Pigeon Creek; A Children's Story Collection; The Golden Sparrow; Buddy and Rambo: The Orphaned Raccoons; Outdoor Adventures; The Arkansas River Monster* collection, and *Do Pets go to Heaven?* This could soon change, however, as he has recently written several others.

The author became a member of *Hoosier Outdoor Writers* in 1993, where he has won several awards from them in their annual writing contest. He has also been a guest speaker for the *Boy Scouts, Daughters of the American Revolution, Teachers Reading Counsel, Kiwanis Club*, and at several schools, libraries, and churches.

Ken has been an outdoor columnist and contributing editor for several newspapers and magazines: *Ohio Valley Sportsman, Kentucky Woods and Waters, Southern Indiana Outdoors, Fur-Fish-Game, Wild Outdoor World, Mid-West Outdoors,* and a hard cover book titled *From the Field.* He has written for the *Boonville Standard, Perry County News, Newburgh Register and Chandler Post.* He has had poems published locally and nationally. One titled *The Stranger* went to missionaries around the world. The poem, *Princess,* was also published locally and nationally, and won honorable mention in a national contest. His best-loved poem is *Condemned* and has been published by the tens of thousands. Nearly every single poem he has written is in his book, *Poems from my Heart.*

Ken has worked for an Evansville, Indiana, television station where he had outdoor news segments aired that he wrote, directed, and edited. He also had film clips that were aired on the national television shows *Real TV* and *Animal Planet.* At this time, he has several short videos on YouTube and on GodTube.

Studying nature since childhood, he is a self-taught ornithologist and a conservationist. In 2009, he became founder and president of the *Golden Sparrow Nature Society*, the name of which was chosen because of his first published book. Ken loves to share his knowledge and love of nature, and it has been said that he is a walking encyclopedia on birds and animals. Because of this, he recently published an E-book titled *Birds and Animals of Southern Indiana*. It has over 300 photos of birds and animals, most of which he photographed himself. He frequently updates it with new photos.

He has followed his dream of being a writer since 1978 and now lives in a cabin in the woods. Being an individualist, he cleared the land, dug a well by hand and built the house himself, which uses only solar electric. He even wrote a book titled *Solar Electric: How does that work?*

Comments or questions on the author's work can be left on his Facebook page at: **Kenneth Edward Barnes.** All of Ken's books can also be seen on his **Author Page** at Amazon.

Other Books by the Author

(My cabin in the woods)

Fictional Novels

1: The Mammoth Slayers
2: The Mammoth Slayers: Last Clan of Neanderthals
3: The Mammoth Slayers: The Last Neanderthal
4: The Mammoth Slayers: Rise of the Cro-Magnons
5: The Mammoth Slayers: The Final Chapter
6: The Mammoth Slayers: The Resurrection
7: The Mammoth Slayers: The Prequel
8: The Arkansas River Monster
9: The Return of the Arkansas River Monster
10: The Capture of the Arkansas River Monster
11: The Last Arkansas River Monster
12: The Arkansas River Monster: The Complete Series
13: Into the West

14: The Black Widow
15: Betrayed
16: In Search of a Golden Sparrow
17: The Day That Time Stood Still
18: Madam President
19: To Keep a Secret (Unpublished right now)
20: Ransom (Unpublished right now)

Non-fiction Novels

21: Life Along Little Pigeon Creek
22: The Long Pond Road
23: A Cabin in the Woods
24: Barnestorming the Outdoors: Revised Edition
25: Kenneth Edward Barnes: An Autobiography
26: Saving Wildlife

Novels and Novelettes for Children

27: The Invasion of the Dregs
28: The Creature of O'Minee
29: Kenny's Children's Stories
30: Children's Stories II
31: Plays for Children
32: Buddy and Rambo: The Orphaned Raccoons

Books of Faith

33: A Biblical Mystery: Christians need to become a Jew:
What does this mean?
34: A Day Appointed
35: A House Divided: This is why Donald Trump won the
election

Books Available as E-books only

www.ingramcontent.com/pod-product-compliance
Lightning Source LLC
Chambersburg PA
CBHW071405280526
45787CB00001B/441